The Religion of the Day

Prime Matters

University of Mary Press

First published in 2023

Published in the United States of America
by University of Mary Press
7500 University Drive
Bismarck, ND 58504
www.umary.edu

ISBN: 978-1-7348826-5-0

Nihil Obstat & Imprimatur

+ The Most Reverend David D. Kagan, D.D., P.A., J.C.L
Bishop of Bismarck
21 August 2023

The *Nihil Obstat* and *Imprimatur* are official declarations that a book or pamphlet is free of doctrinal or moral error. No implication is contained therein that those who granted them agree with the content or statements expressed.

Design: Brady J. Braun

Printed in Canada

Cover Image

LA FÊTE DE LA RAISON À NOTRE-DAME DE PARIS LE 10 NOVEMBRE 1793

by Charles-Louis Müller, 1878
Oil on canvas, 188 x 227 cm
Musée Saint Croix, Poitiers, France

Table of Contents

Introduction

It Isn't Christendom Any More

To be a reflective Catholic is always to be a Catholic rather than *something else. So, Augustine was a Catholic* rather than *a Manichean or a Neoplatonist; Pascal was a Catholic* rather than *a skeptic or a Cartesian; Maritain was a Catholic* rather than *a materialist or a Bergsonian. In what they affirm Scripturally, in the creeds, and liturgically, there is that which is the same for Catholics of every generation. But the denials that are the counterparts to those affirmations vary with time, place, and culture. So how is it with us here now?*

— Alasdair McIntyre[1]

IT IS POSSIBLE to do many Catholic things, and yet not have a Catholic mind. This is especially true in our post-Christian age.

It is to be expected. As the ideas that provide the grounding of a culture shift, many people will continue their usual religious practices even as, without noting it, their view of the world is subtly changing. This is not meant as a critique of any individual person. It is simply the dynamic of a time in which the Christian faith is being abandoned and replaced by another very different and quite potent way of viewing the world.

1 "Catholic Instead of What?"

What is required is a response. Such a response begins by recognizing and describing the cultural shift, an explanation that was offered in an earlier book, *From Christendom to Apostolic Mission.* But an effective response also requires a more sophisticated analysis of the new way of viewing the world that is replacing the Christian one – what we, borrowing from John Henry Newman, are calling the "Religion of the Day." This book is an attempt to explain the religion of the day and provide principles for responding to it.

Before we proceed with a proper introduction to this work, a bit of background. The first book in what we have begun to think of as a series, *From Christendom to Apostolic Mission,* published in 2020 by University of Mary Press, was in its essence the product of an ongoing conversation over many years among a set of friends and colleagues. The text itself was compiled by a central scribe for the sake of maintaining a consistent voice and to avoid the inevitable drawbacks of the work of a committee – such as over-nuanced prose, rhetorical inconsistency, and the over-qualification of just about every claim – all of which result in the loss of argumentative force. Committee work convinces no one. The overwhelmingly positive reception of the first book seems to justify the same editorial strategy for this one.

Though there is a central scribe, the overarching argument of *From Christendom to Apostolic Mission* is a shared one. It is the product of many minds – some living and some dead. This, at least in part, accounts for its success. For many readers, the argument of the book was confirming what they had encountered themselves and intuitively already knew, but that came to life when explained succinctly and clearly. A living conversation is just that – alive.

The argument of that earlier work, for those who have not read it, was that our culture in the West is no longer Christian in any

real sense. It certainly retains some Christian elements in its social artifacts – there are, of course, still Christian churches on many corners in America – but as the foundational source for shaping the broader culture, Christianity has been for the most part displaced by a new set of first principles, a new constellation of dogmas, and a new story. We called this process the developing of a new "imaginative vision." The book offered some insights into how the Church could best think about this post-Christian reality and how it might approach its mission of evangelization and faith formation. Rather than thinking of ourselves as living in a Christendom time, a time when the dominant meaning-shaping story of the society is Christian, we should think of ourselves as living in a time not unlike that of the early Christians – an apostolic age.

It is especially in times of significant social or cultural change that new responses are needed to deal with new challenges to faith and human life. Older formulations, effective in their time, do not have the potency they once did. In military circles, there is a concern to be sure that an army is not "fighting the last war," using technologies or tactics that worked well in their day but that no longer meet the demands of a new situation. Something similar could be said of the Church's ongoing strategies for bringing God's rescue to a fallen world and maintaining strength and purity of faith among its own members.

Such times of significant change, times when the tectonic plates of the society are on the move, tend to be marked by a greater degree of corruption within Church authorities and structures and a greater number of Christians who either lose their faith entirely or live it in a half-hearted way. This is partly because of the influx of new ideas that have not yet been sufficiently understood, digested, and countered, and partly because when older strategies are not working well,

it becomes easier for those pursuing them to lose their focus and to embrace false or problematic ways of meeting their responsibilities and living out their faith. Such times of change are also characterized by dynamic movements of Christian renewal and new developments responding to new challenges, and they are always accompanied by the gift of impressive saints who help lead the Church into the next stage of its perennial struggle.

So we need to move to an apostolic stance and devise strategies that begin with the understanding that we are in a non-Christian environment.

1. Not a Blueprint

But we are deliberately not providing here a blueprint for a new apostolic program.

That is largely because we do not think that there is simply one program or new model for evangelization or faith formation that will act as a cure-all. We hold this for two reasons.

First, in times of dramatic cultural change, it has been the consistent testimony of history that the Church adopts any number of strategies that emerge in different places under various leaders, with different if related charisms, each of which in its own way charts a path forward. For example, in nineteenth-century increasingly post-Christian France, one of the notable reasons that the number and variety of saints, movements, apostolates, and renewal efforts were powerful and effective during that time of apostasy was precisely because they were not coordinated. We suspect that the same dynamic will hold true in our own age. It is a process that is already happening. In the West, in places where the post-Christian development is most advanced, one can look to a large number of new apostolates and movements, as well as programs for parish renewal,

diocesan evangelization, and ecclesial efforts, all making their way against steady headwinds, slowly and maybe not in large numbers. These are Benedict XVI's "creative minorities." If the past is any indicator, such sources of renewal, small but faithful, are likely to become wellsprings of significant transformation as they are given time to grow. It is for the Lord to decide which ones will prosper and which will fail in days ahead, but it seems best that they all have room to follow the inspiration of the Holy Spirit as he guides each and to allow them to offer the leadership and inspiration we need in this era of massive change.

Second, we are convinced that one of the temptations of our time, as will be noted later, is our readiness to look for techniques that will guarantee success. We are tempted to want a program that we can put into operation, a set of practices and protocols about whose effectiveness we can be confident, a technique that will be universally applicable. It is true that we need to find specific strategies that will enable us to express, live, and spread our faith. But if we settle too quickly on a particular program or technique, the apparatus we have so confidently constructed will often lack the flexibility needed to respond to the multiplicity of "facts on the ground" and will tantalizingly absolve us of the difficult task of dealing with the uniqueness and complexity of what we are facing. It would be a case of falling prey to a mode of thinking that is characteristic of the dominant modern religion. More important for us is to get a firm hold on the fundamental principles that should inform whatever specific strategies we develop. Once our principles are sound, we can turn our energy to developing effective strategies founded on those principles that will suit the demands and possibilities of our highly complex and differing situations.

So no blueprint. What then does the book propose?

2. The Three-Front Christian Battle

God in Christ came among us to wage a spiritual battle and, in every age since the time of its founding by Christ, the Church has been engaged in a kind of three-front war. On one front, Christians fight an external battle against the unbelief of a fallen world; a second front is an internal battle against disloyalty and corruption among Church members; and most importantly, the third front is a fight against the darkness and unbelief of one particular member of the Church: namely, ourselves. Much of the nature of that battle is the same in every age: *Jesus Christ is the same yesterday, today, and forever* (Heb 13:8), and human nature, despite what many current philosophies want to suggest, is fundamentally constant. These perennial realities mean that the revealed truths of the Faith apply to all of humanity at all times from every race, culture, nation, and people. Yet it is also true that the terrain of that graced battle – the specific strategies necessary to stand for truth and to win the allegiance of non-believers to Christ, the particular forms of internal Church corruption, and the nature of the lies and temptations that afflict individual Christians – changes from age to age and place to place. In the deepest sense the Church does not change. In another sense the Church, at least that small part of it currently living on earth, changes constantly, and has been remarkably proficient at adapting its unchanging truths to the changing human environments it inhabits. If we look through the two-thousand-year history of the Church, we can see that many of the most beloved and characteristic expressions of our faith were inspired by the Holy Spirit engaging the battle for truth in a particular cultural context.

3. The Structure of the Book

Broadly speaking, this book addresses the question of how the Church can best negotiate the religion of the day along these three main fronts.

First: We think that responding to our current situation demands gaining a better understanding of the religion of the day, both to discover how it has affected us as Christians and to learn how best to address it in our apostolic endeavors. Chapters 1, 2, and 3 – entitled "The Religion of the Day," "Twelve Aspects of Modern Progressive Religion," and "Some Further Notes on Progressive, Neo-Gnostic Religion" – attempt to formulate a basic answer to the question posed by Alasdair McIntyre at the head of this introduction: what is the religion we need to be converted *out of,* if we are to be truly converted to Christ? These chapters deal especially with the first battle front mentioned, the external spiritual battle. In order to be able to devise effective strategies, it is imperative that we have a sound understanding of the basic principles that underlie the increasingly influential religion vying with Christ for the hearts and minds of the people of our time. *From Christendom to Apostolic Mission* offered a description of that religion, but it has seemed important, arising from conversations many of us have had across the country based on the book, to provide a deeper unpacking of the modern imaginative vision for Christian leaders, both lay and ecclesial.

The particular usefulness of these chapters may be found in their attempt to integrate the many analyses of the current imaginative vision both on the popular and on the academic level into a clear, but not overly simplified, whole. We believe that by approaching the many ideologies of the day from the perspective of first principles and fundamental convictions, we can identify consistent underlying threads – dogmas – that unite them. Those threads will be described

in more detail in the text itself. Our overall descriptive label for the religion of the day is to gather it under the general heading of *neo-Gnosticism*. While this modifier requires some explanation, it provides a useful framework for sorting through the often jargon-laden, inflammatory, and frankly manipulative language that characterizes modern political and cultural discourse.

Some readers may find these chapters a bit challenging; there is some necessary background in intellectual and cultural history that goes into unpacking these ideas. Nonetheless we think it is worth including this foray into the intellectual background of modern religion. To be a Christian in any age is to believe the Gospel *instead of* some alternative. Especially for those in positions of leadership and responsibility, the better we understand the alternative religion, the better prepared we will be to meet its challenges and to serve those for whom we are responsible.

Second: The book attempts to address a sometimes inadequate view of the Church that many of us tend to hold and to re-emphasize certain important truths of the Faith. This topic is covered in Chapter 4, entitled "Catching All the Diseases of the World." Because the religion of the day is fundamentally utopian, Christians of our time can be tempted to view the Church using a vaguely utopian lens. It has been a source of shock to many Christians that the false religious ideas of our age have found their way into the Church itself – including at the higher levels of leadership. How should we understand this? We argue that far from being a surprising exception, the fact that the counter-gospel of the day has penetrated the Church is typical of Church history. The Church historically has always had to fight the battle against the intellectual disease of the day (if you will permit the analogy) within her own walls, in order to develop the cure and make it available to the wider culture. This chapter is

most pertinent to the second battlefront, the fight against corruption inside the Church. A number of us have had the opportunity to present this argument in public presentations. Based on the response, I am sure that for many readers this will be the most immediately resonant section of the book.

Third: Chapters 5 and 6 engage the battlefront that is the most decisive for the majority of Christians: the struggle to live as fully converted and faithful followers of Christ. Chapter 5, "The Battle for Deeper Conversion," looks at ways that serious Christians can be taught and formed by the religion of the day rather than by Christ and can unwittingly take on attitudes and modes of behavior that mirror that false religion. Chapter 6, "The Winning Stance," outlines a posture for the Church in the apostolic age we are increasingly inhabiting. One does not need to be an apocalyptic prophet to note that the Church in our time is once again being offered the burden and the glory of being confessors and maybe martyrs for the cause of faithfulness to our beloved Christ. In this we will find ourselves closer to the Church of the first centuries than to the Church during the long centuries of Christendom.

4. A Personal Note

There is, regrettably, an inherent danger awaiting any work that takes up the question of the ideologies of the day; namely, that it will be read as nothing more than a political statement. This is no doubt true in any age of contested political visions, but it is also true because the religion of the day focuses exclusively on this world, and the question of politics necessarily and by design takes center stage. But this is not the Church's vision of reality, nor is it the main interest of this book. The ideas presented here no doubt have certain implications for modern politics, but the essay is not written for that purpose. The

tone is deliberately descriptive, and disrespectful rhetoric has been avoided even when making judgments of various ideas.

This is an important point – and leads me to a personal conviction that I do not necessarily ascribe to any other contributor to the conversations that gave birth to this book. The ideas that have captured the minds of so many people, especially our young people – no matter how inconsistent, falsifiable, or prone to emotive exaggeration – are held with deep conviction and have been arrived at for compelling reasons. For example, while I do not hold with an interpretation of the world that reduces everything to a particular injustice based on race or sexual preference, I take the alienation and injustices that give rise to these interpretations very seriously. And I think that they deserve a serious answer. Such an answer to the problems we all share – personally and as a society – is what Christianity provides, better than any alternative. It offers an answer to the alienation we all experience, an ultimate solution to the injustice so obvious to anyone who takes an honest look at our society. Yet in order for the Christian answer to be heard and taken seriously, Christians need to take seriously what others see and experience. Ours is a world under the curse of the Fall, in fundamental rupture with our loving Creator. But it is also a world in the process of being redeemed. And thus, we offer the world not simply *an* answer to our serious problems, but *the only* answer: Jesus Christ.

Finally, it is worth noting that this essay echoes many voices who have been involved in sorting out the important questions it treats, and there are different modes of speaking, emphases or nuances that some might prefer to put differently. Still, as was true of *From Christendom to Apostolic Mission,* the overall argument here is a shared one. This book is offered in the same spirit as the first, encouraging those who are thinking seriously about the issues it addresses to

promote, adapt, or rearticulate its content as they find helpful. The hope is to further a living conversation, not to end it. If it sparks a strong response, of whatever kind, all those involved in the project will find their effort well rewarded.

Dr. Jonathan Reyes
Senior Vice President for Strategic Outreach & Senior Advisor
Knights of Columbus

I

The Religion of the Day

"It is doubtful that we can consider the Enlightenment as an age basically irreligious and inimical to religion.... The strongest intellectual forces of the Enlightenment do not lie in its rejection of belief but rather in the new form of faith which it proclaims, and in the new form of religion which it embodies."

— Ernst Cassirer[2]

"History began when humans invented god, and it will end when humans become gods."

— Yuval Harari[3]

1. Our Modern Religious Age

WE OFTEN SPEAK of our age, especially in the West, as increasingly non-religious: the so-called rise of the "nones." If religion is defined as an ordered system of rites and practices that govern our relationship to the supernatural world and teach us our duties toward God, then to say that our society has been growing less religious, often defiantly so, is obviously true. But religion can also be usefully

2 *The Philosophy of the Enlightenment*

3 *Homo Deus: A History of Tomorrow*

understood as the particular set of beliefs and practices that a person or a society holds in order to provide a meaningful vision and narrative for life. In that sense of the term, there can be religions (admittedly not very good ones) that deny the existence of God and the supernatural world and still function for all practical purposes as religions. Humans are inveterate meaning-seeking beings. We are unable to live and function, personally or societally, if we do not have some sense of why we are alive and what we are living for. We need to settle on a way of looking at the world and our place in it that provides hope for the future, that organizes our moral life, and that points out our path forward. Such a narrative of meaning is never merely scientific or informational. It involves a personal commitment to a set of beliefs and moral doctrines and also an embrace of dogmas that cannot be simply proven and that are held with a tenacity alien to the mere acquisition of information. Time-bound beings that we are, we cannot live without hope for the future, and hope demands a narrative of meaning. A narrative of meaning necessarily brings about a personal engagement with what it proposes. Attack a person's hope and you attack the basis of that person's life; hence the deep personal commitment that characterizes religious belief.

If religion is understood in this sense, it follows that every person is to some degree religious by nature: everyone is seeking a meaningful story. Some will be highly committed to their religion while others will be less so. But even the less zealous are resting their lives on a vision of meaning, often unconsciously, which can be seen by the way any person goes into crisis when the narrative by which they have been living loses its cogency.

According to the above understanding of religion, we in the West are living in a highly religious age. Dogmatically held faiths promising salvation, secular gospels of various kinds, are widely held

and are being relentlessly propagated all around us. The question therefore arises: what is the belief system, the religious vision, that is displacing Christianity as the assumed narrative by which our post-Christian, modern societies live? And what is the religion that we need to be converted *out of*, if we are to be fully converted to the Christian faith?

2. The Primal Heresy

In the face of the often-bewildering complexity of modern philosophies and ideologies, it might be thought that there is no one religious vision attempting to displace Christianity. The old adage has it that "truth is simple, but error is manifold." Untangling the currents of modern thought and belief is no easy matter. Yet our contention is that in the midst of these many differing views, there is a fundamental unity to an emerging and increasingly dominant religious vision, a unity found not in the specifics of doctrines and practices, but in the deep structure, the first principles, upon which those many variants are built. The "religion of the day" does not go by a single name, and different observers have called it many different things. A descriptive and overly cumbersome name for it might be: "Modern Neo-Gnostic Progressive Utopian Revolutionary Religion." For the sake of simplicity, it will mainly be referred to here as "Progressive religion."

Our argument is that the religion that has been battling for the last few centuries to displace Christianity is a uniquely potent form of a heresy that has dogged the Church like a dark shadow from its beginnings: the heresy of Gnosticism.[4] Modern Gnostic religion is

[4] The term "gnosticism" is derived from a Greek word for "knowledge" or "awareness": γνῶσις, gnōsis.

different in many of its aspects from Gnostic heresies of the early centuries and from medieval Gnostic systems. But though it is flying under new colors, the spiritual roots and the deep structure of the Gnostic religious attitude remain. That structure, what could be called the Gnostic turn of mind, will be explained below.[5]

Many observers have pointed to a Gnostic strain in modern thinking. Among them have been Popes John Paul II, Benedict XVI, and Francis; theologians Henri de Lubac and Hans Urs van Balthasar; and various others including Hans Jonas, Eric Voegelin, Martin Buber, Harold Bloom, Agosto Del Noce, Christopher Lasch, Remi Brague, Roger Scruton, Robert George, and Ross Douthat. That there is a strong neo-Gnostic current in modernity seems clear and can be taken as a given. Sorting out what that influence means, where it has come from, why and how it has developed, and how it might be confronted are complex and important tasks beyond the aim of this discussion. We are not engaging here in a detailed study of the history of ideas, or a sociological account of modern culture, useful and important as such efforts might be. Our aim is more immediately practical. We hope to identify the spiritual principles and underlying assumptions of modern neo-Gnostic religious belief as they tend to be assumed and held by ourselves and the majority of

---

5 "Gnosticism" is a word one would prefer to avoid, if only because it can be taken to mean so many different things. The term most often refers to a group of religious sects that arose in the first Christian centuries, often depicted as granting secret knowledge to a chosen few while teaching that the material world is of little value. The study of the ancient Gnostics still holds much of interest, but their intricate doctrines and convoluted myths have little resonance for most modern minds, and the term "Gnosticism" falls strangely on modern ears. There has been a large and growing literature examining recently discovered Gnostic writings and addressing the relationship between Gnosticism and early Christianity. Whatever the merits of that scholarship and the various debates it has produced, the hope here is to sidestep them entirely. We are less concerned to come up with a neat way of categorizing philosophical schools of thought and religious phenomena than with understanding the way the dogmas of modern religion take root in the minds and hearts of their believers, many of whom are anything but philosophers.

the people around us, such that their dynamics can be better understood and that those who have been influenced by them, including many within the Church, can be more effectively converted to the Christian Gospel.

Gnosticism has been called "the primal heresy within the Christian worldview to which all subsequent heresies return."[6] The arrival of some form of Gnostic religion seems to be the inevitable accompaniment to Christianity wherever it succeeds in gaining significant cultural influence. Due to the relationship between Christian faith and Gnostic alterations to the faith, a paradoxical situation arises. The more deeply a society has been influenced by Christianity, the more likely it is that it will produce Gnostic variants, and the more potent those variants will be. It is not surprising therefore to find that the last few centuries have seen the development of very potent forms of neo-Gnostic faith, given that Western society and culture have been so deeply influenced by Christianity. Gnostic religion is the classic case of Christianity gone awry.

To call the religious narrative of our society "neo-Gnostic" is not to suggest that the majority of Americans or Europeans are card-carrying Gnostics. Just as only a minority of individuals were consistent and fervent Christians in times of Christendom, so in the neo-Gnostic atmosphere of our time only a minority are active and self-declared followers of one or another Progressive belief system. Even those who are consciously pursuing a Gnostic scheme of salvation seldom call it by that name. But even when unacknowledged and unperceived, neo-Gnostic belief increasingly provides the substrata, the first principles of meaning and moral life, for the majority of moderns.

---

6 Roger Scruton, *Fools, Frauds, & Firebrands*

3. Not a Religion?

An unfortunate aspect of modern Progressive religion is that it is usually not recognized as a dogmatic faith by its devotees. Those who subscribe to one or another of its variants often think of themselves as being noteworthily rational, scientific, and non-religious, even while expressing evident religious behavior, such as their commitment to doctrines and dogmas that are hardly self-evident, their holding to those dogmas with a tenacity incommensurate with their provability, their propensity to seek out fellow-believers who can cooperate in their sacred project and with whom they can experience communion, and their quick vilification of heretics to their faith. The problem with this state of affairs is not the religious nature of their beliefs. It is rather that by denying their own views as religious and therefore as having the quality of dogma, they are unable to exercise the kind of thoughtful investigation of dogma necessary for any intelligently held religious faith, and they are unable to distinguish the kind of knowledge gained by religious assumptions from other kinds of knowledge. They then demand that "religious" considerations be left out of all the questions of the day, not realizing that they are promoting and often coercing the practice of their own religion upon others under the false guise of being religiously neutral.

Some past theorists of modern Progressive belief understood more clearly that they were putting forward a new religion, even when they recognized that it was a secular religion without metaphysics or divinity. The proponents of the radical phase of the French Revolution in 1792 instituted an entirely new calendar, eventually introducing a whole round of religious feasts and enthroning the "goddess reason" in the cathedral of Notre Dame in Paris. Auguste Comte, the nineteenth-century French thinker who is one of the founders of sociology – a significant fact to keep in mind in understanding

the dogmas of modern social science – called for the entire replacement of Christianity by a new faith that he named the "religion of humanity." Comte understood the importance of religious practice in holding together a human society; his new secular faith came complete with high priests, feast days, and ritual celebrations. John Dewey, the influential American philosopher especially important in the area of education, helped author the "Humanist Manifesto," which argued that a new humanistic religion was needed to replace the old supernatural one. It would be an aid to clarity if the more recent proponents of Progressive faiths had the same readiness as Robespierre, Comte, and Dewey to identify themselves as followers of a religion. But it is not hard to see why religious language has been dropped by the proponents of these faiths, since retaining it would mean a problematic encounter with modern democracies that purport to disallow the official establishment of any one religion.

4. The Structure of Modern Progressive Religion

What then is the underlying structure of Progressive religion? What set of principles can give a unity to so many seemingly disparate cultural currents and ideas that we see around us? A modern neo-Gnostic belief system is:

- A scheme of self-initiated salvation;
- that locates the source of the world's evil not in the individual human heart, but in fundamentally corrupted and therefore oppressive structures of human existence, whether spiritual, material, societal, or psychological;
- that promises to radically overcome the evil of the world and the alienation and lack of fulfillment experienced by humans;

- that accomplishes this salvation through escape from or destruction of prevailing structures of oppression, however they may be identified;
- that claims to bring about a new type of human and to inaugurate an entirely new age of freedom that has overcome the past age of oppression;
- and that accomplishes its salvation through the application of some form of specialized technical knowledge (gnosis) gained by human effort.

There is a further spiritual quality of Progressive religion, due to its inner structure:

- Neo-Gnostic belief is essentially, not accidentally, an expression of human pride.

How this set of principles takes shape in modern Progressive religion will be the topic of the next chapter.

G. K. Chesterton once described the Church as a lion-tamer: "It was no flock of sheep the Christian shepherd was leading, but a herd of bulls and tigers, of terrible ideals and devouring doctrines, each one of them strong enough to turn to a false religion and lay waste the world."[7] This has been the tragic trend of Progressive religion: to seize upon the overall narrative of Christianity, to alter it in the direction of self-redemption, and to pursue a destructive course, claiming the dramatic sweep, moral seriousness, and missionary spirit of the Christianity from which it arose and to which it owes most of its potency, even as it lays waste the world.

---

7. *Orthodoxy*

II

Twelve Aspects of Modern Progressive Religion

"Imagine there's no heaven; It's easy if you try.
No hell below us; Above us, only sky.
You may say I'm a dreamer; But I'm not the only one.
I hope someday you'll join us, And the world will be as one."

—John Lennon

1. The Human Tragedy of Alienation

Progressive religion acknowledges the human tragedy of profound alienation from the world, and even from our own being.

MODERN PROGRESSIVE FAITHS, like all Gnostic schemes, begin with the recognition that there is a great deal of evil in the world, and that at an existential level, humans experience deep alienation from their own being, an alienation that cannot be overcome by normal ways of adjusting to life. Progressive religion is rooted in this common human experience, and it gains much of its attraction by appealing to the sense of alienation that we all experience. In this it resonates with and borrows from Christianity and has found imaginative depth in the Christian view of the profound dislocation we all experience because of sin and exile from Eden.

The happy-go-lucky type who thinks that all is going swimmingly and that life is a picnic is not a likely recruit for a Progressive religious cause. Nor is the apathetic person who thinks that it's really not worth bothering much about bad things. More to the point is the common sentiment of those who want to "make the world a better place," or the bumper sticker admonition: "If you're not outraged, you're not paying attention."

It might be thought that the experience of alienation from the existing world has been a universal religious starting point, but that would not be accurate. Polytheistic nature religions, for example, are founded on the idea that human life is coterminous with the natural (which includes the spiritual) world and that the point of religion is to help humans find their proper place in the cycle of living and dying. Examples of that type of belief would include the religions of ancient Egypt, Mesopotamia, Mesoamerica, and India. A modern, sanitized expression of this religious attitude can be found in the lyrics of the song from the movie *The Lion King*, "The Circle of Life." Such religions provide considerable consistency and stability over millennia for the civilizations founded on them. In imitating the rhythms of the natural world, they tend – like nature itself – to be both beautiful and cruel. In addition, some philosophies, like the Confucian and the Taoist, provide sophisticated pictures of the continuity of humanity with the universe and point out a path to harmony and peace in the midst of it. Progressive religion instead follows Christianity in breaking with this way of thinking, insisting that the condition of the current world is seriously flawed, and that the last thing one wants to do is to conform to its corruptions.

2. Salvation is Possible

Progressive believers hold that salvation, meaning escape from the current state of alienation, is an attainable goal.

Progressive religion is not fatalistic: it offers a salvific vision, one that engenders a hope that all, or at least most, of our suffering can be ended. Against the backdrop of an unjust and suffering world, it puts forward a scheme of salvation that promises to overcome human alienation. In this again it mirrors Christianity and borrows much of its narrative punch from the Christian doctrine of salvation. Prior to Christianity, most religions held a murky and ambiguous view of the afterlife, usually a land of shadow like Hades or Sheol, or a state of near non-existence like Nirvana. Even when good things were expected, they were envisioned within the limits of earthly human happiness, like the Happy Hunting Ground, or the Norse Valhalla, which itself was one day to fall to its enemies. But Christianity brought to humanity a majestic hope: *What no eye has seen and what no ear has heard* (1 Cor 2:9), the complete healing and glorification of humanity in eternal bliss. Progressive religion has imbibed and digested that hope and has worked it into its own imaginative vision. An exhilarating promise of freedom from personal alienation and the perfection of human society, not in some distant future state but in the world as it now exists, beckons the progressive believer and offers a strong incentive, especially in young and ardent minds, to accomplish that perfected state through faith and self-sacrifice.

3. The Transformation of Our Humanity

The salvation offered by Progressive religion promises not only escape from evil, but the transformation of our current humanity.

Here, too, Progressive religion borrows from Christianity. Christians have held that in Christ we are to become *partakers of*

the divine nature (2 Pet 1:4). Christians are not merely brought to a place of healthy and happy human existence according to the limits and possibilities of our current state of being. We are to be transformed beyond what we can now imagine. Christ is the new Adam, the "firstborn" of a regenerated and divinized human race (Col 1:3). Progressive religion promises a similar human transformation, one that resonates deeply with our God-given desire for transcendence.

Because Progressive belief claims to surpass the current constraints of humanity, it always places great importance on the notion of freedom, another Christian word with a long and notable pedigree. Christians have understood themselves to have been set free by Christ and delivered from oppressive forces: sin and guilt, death, slavery to the devil, and internal disharmony. Progressive religion also embraces the idea of freedom, but it changes its meaning and points it in different directions. According to Progressive religion, we can be set free from whatever limits us in the current age of the world, whether that limit is economic, social, spiritual, physical, psychological, or sexual, and we can experience a noble expansion of our being as we freely determine who and what we will be. Freedom is an incantatory word in all Progressive forms of faith, not as something to be achieved through a road of discipline and the development of virtue according to a divine pattern but by breaking the perceived bonds of oppression that limit the self-creative process.

4. The Source of Alienation Not Within Us

For the Progressive believer, the cause of our alienation is to be found not within ourselves, but in the existing (dis)order of an evil world.

To this point in the discussion, Progressive religion and Christianity can be seen to have many common starting points: the dark experience of human alienation, the obvious evils of the world, the

promise of salvation, and the transformation of human life. But here Progressive faiths make a decisive break with Christianity and embrace a principle that represents the entire subversion of the Christian account of reality. When Progressive believers look for the reason behind the alienation we so painfully experience, they find the cause of that alienation not within themselves, but rather in some aspect of the external world. Like Christians, they know that the only way life will get better is if something radically changes. Unlike Christians, they hold that what needs to radically change is emphatically not *me.* Here we encounter the most important founding principle in all the many variants of Progressive faith: *the denial of the doctrine of the Fall.* It is not *we* who have fallen, by choosing evil and inflicting on ourselves a moral wound that has laid us open to being enslaved by powerful dark forces. It is instead *the world* that has been poisoned, or perhaps that was created evil from the start, and we find our good selves trapped in the world's evil oppressive structures. According to Progressive religion, we will overcome our alienation when we destroy those evil structures and remake the world on a new and good pattern. A classic expression of this attitude is found at the beginning of Jean-Jacques Rousseau's influential work, *The Social Contract:* "Man is born free, and everywhere he is in chains." This is almost the exact reverse of the Christian understanding: that humans are born into moral and spiritual slavery, and only in Christ can we be set free.

This founding principle of Progressive religion – the denial of original sin, the refusal to find the source of human evil in the individual human heart – points to the prideful turn at the core of all Progressive faiths. Most of the world's religions have demanded a measure of humility, involving submission to a cosmic order as a way of healing the human soul and attaining to divine harmonies. The Progressive believer begins with the doctrine that the self is free of

evil and free of guilt, except to the degree that it has been contaminated by the external evil of a darkened world. It then ascribes all evil, including personal moral evil, to an external someone or something else. "Not my fault!" is the universal Progressive religious mantra.

The quintessential Gnostic turn was taken by Eve in the Garden. The nature of Eve's temptation points to its attractive power. Eve was drawn to the fruit of the tree of the Knowledge of Good and Evil because she saw that *it was good for food, and that it was a delight to the eyes, and that the tree was to be desired to make one wise* (Gen 3:6). Something in her God-created nature responded to what the fruit promised. She felt that it was suited to her, and that possession of it would move her toward her true destiny. Her moral failure was in attempting to seize for herself what in the nature of things could only come to her as a gift from her Creator. In their pride, she and Adam attempted to accomplish the creation of their own being, and they destroyed themselves in the process. Christ, the new Adam, when faced with a similar situation, did not count the greatness of his being *something to be grasped* like the fruit in the Garden. Instead, *he emptied himself*, trusting in the One who was the true source of life, and as a result he received his high destiny from God's hand (Phil 2).

Ancient Gnostics inhabited the world of Greek philosophical thought and fed upon it for much of their mythic structure. They assumed the existence of a spiritual world and the reality of the human soul, and they viewed materiality unfavorably. They sometimes went so far as to say that the material world was created by the devil. Salvation was thus to be found in the flight of the good spiritual soul from the shackles of material oppression. For the ancient Gnostics material creation itself was the Fall.

With the teaching of Genesis that the world and everything in it was created "good" by the High God, and under centuries of the

influence of the powerful Christian doctrine of sacramentality – the sanctification of the material world through the Incarnation – the evil ascribed by the ancient Gnostics to materiality has become less imaginatively plausible. Most modern forms of Progressive religion accept the materiality of the world. It is not materiality itself, but the current structures of the material and social worlds that are evil and need to be rejected. The Progressive believer gains salvation not by escaping materiality entirely, though some forms of transhumanism seem to point that way, but by effecting a radical change in the way the material world is ordered. Though it is not always apparent on the surface, every Progressive religion harbors a profound hatred for the world as it currently exists and a corresponding anger toward the entrenched but evil order that it believes is the cause of human alienation and injustice.

5. Tragic Hostility to God

Progressive religion necessarily and tragically leads to hostility toward God.

By its own inner logic, Progressive religion's anger toward the existing world arrives, by a sad necessity, at hostility toward the possibility of a God who created it and who stands behind its evil order. Progressive religion inevitably results in hatred for God, though it can take time for that hatred to manifest itself, and many who embrace Progressive belief are not fully aware of this innate tendency of their religious vision. Among Progressive believers who still call themselves Christians, this hostility is expressed not so much by denying the existence of God outright as by rejecting God's revelation of himself and by changing the glorious and awe-inspiring Deity into a harmless figure who does not interfere with Progressive self-realization. God is thus effectively destroyed, even while appearances are kept up and a sentimental attachment to the forms of Christianity continue to

offer a certain ballast to life. Irenaeus wrote that the essence of all Gnostic sects was blasphemy against the Creator[8], a remark that is also valid for neo-Gnostic Progressive faiths, including those that fly under Christian colors.

Examples of radical hostility to the existing order of the world and a resulting atheistic bent, whether overt or latent, are found throughout the history of modernity's neo-Gnostic religious movements. There has been a succession of attempts to break decisively with what were perceived as the evil structures of existence, and as each attempt has failed to overcome the depths of human alienation, a further and deeper change has been insisted upon. Expressions of this kind of developing hostility can be seen in the Enlightened eighteenth-century *philosophes'* historical narrative that viewed the Middle Ages as a time of unrelieved darkness (e.g., Condorcet); in the French revolutionary attitude to the *Ancien Régime* and the attempt to remake society by abolishing the nobility and radically altering the political and cultural order; in the Marxist hostility toward bourgeois capitalism and the drive for a revolutionary change in the economic and therefore class order; in the Freudian angst toward the domination of the superego and the structure of the human psyche; in the radical feminist hatred of patriarchy as embodying an oppressive order of gender; in the hostility of the proponents of sexual liberation toward marriage and family and a "heteronormative" understanding of sexual life; in the anger promoted by variants of critical theory toward what is called "privilege"; in the anti-human sentiment apparent in some strains of the ecological movement; and perhaps the most sweeping of all, in the transhumanist contempt for the physical and mental order of humans and the hope to remake humanity from the ground

---

8 *Against Heresies*, x.3

up. Each of these successive (and sometimes concurrent) expressions of neo-Gnostic faith shares the same fundamental terrain, and each attempts a profound structural change, borrowing categories of thought from each other in differing combinations. It is natural that participants in these various movements often feel an elective affinity to one another. Voltaire's famous cry against the Church, "*Écrasez l'infâme!*" ("Crush the loathsome thing!") is the battle cry of Progressive believers against the order of the current world and against the God who is perceived as somehow standing behind it, as they insist on the utter annihilation of the structure of an oppressive system as the necessary prerequisite for the new age of freedom to come.

The aggressive atheism of most modern neo-Gnostic movements is often viewed by their followers as the logical outcome of scientific or social-scientific thinking. Marx called his brand of communism "scientific socialism," and his followers have continued to clothe their religious assumptions in the esoteric language of pseudo-science. Auguste Comte insisted that the world had *progressed* from a religious, through a philosophic, and finally to a scientific understanding of the world by which metaphysics was shown to be non-existent. Many propounders of scientism, from Thomas Huxley in the nineteenth century to recent figures like Richard Dawkins, have tried to make the dubious claim that there has been a warfare between religion and science, and that science – by which they mean hard, demonstrable fact – has shown religion to be untrue. But the atheistic basis of Progressive religion is not a conclusion coming at the end of philosophic or scientific inquiry; it is the implicitly assumed but often unconscious starting point of the religion. If a creator-God were to exist, the Progressive dogma that humans will find their freedom and dignity through self-creation would be impossible to maintain. Historically, practical atheism has been both the shrouded

beginning and the final result toward which all Progressive religious schemes tend.

6. A High but Ambiguous Moral Call

Progressive religion issues a high but ambiguous moral call.

Progressive religion sounds a bracing moral call and claims to occupy the moral high ground in whatever cause it takes up. Progressive believers are very aware of the suffering that comes from injustice and, thinking themselves to be fighters against the world's evil, they can be ready to make personal sacrifices for what they believe. This stance of moral seriousness in the face of perceived injustice and the strong commitment to defeating evil and bringing about a better world, a quality originally borrowed from Christianity, gives the Progressive religious narrative much of its attractiveness, especially among young and idealistic spirits. But because Progressive religion denies the Fall, and therefore leaves its adherents unchastened by the realization that all people, including themselves, are sinners in desperate need of forgiveness, it tends to produce an unfortunate but inevitable collective attitude of moral superiority. Pharisaic self-righteousness is the sad but predictable result of the Progressive attempt at moral reform, even among individuals who are not personally inclined to self-conceit.

Christians, who have embraced a philosophy of perennial truths and values, can often be confused or seduced by variants of Progressive faith because Progressive campaigns often attack situations that are genuinely morally problematic. Whether it be the depredations of the aristocracy in eighteenth-century France, or the sad plight of workers in nineteenth-century Europe, or the evil blot of slavery and Jim Crow visited on blacks by whites in America, or aspects of inequality between women and men that have needed reform in a

modern technological society, Progressive religions often begin with an assault upon real injustice (though not always, as can be seen in the Progressive attack on the unborn). Christians, moved by a concern for justice, can be recruited to a neo-Gnostic cause, not perceiving that the proposed remedies often run directly counter to the wisdom of Christ. However much they may seem to coincide, there is a radical difference between the Christian call to love the poor and the modern resentment of poverty, or the Christian concern to care for the elderly and the prevalent hatred for mortality and the ravages of age, or the Christian impulse to aid the sick and the neo-Gnostic indignation toward disease. But, although they are in reality poles apart, the disparity is often unclear at the outset. The deeper principles of the two faiths only emerge as time passes, when it becomes apparent that poverty cannot simply be overcome, or that disease and old age cannot be entirely conquered. At that point the logic of the Progressive mindset makes itself felt, and an insistent call is sounded to eliminate the poor, to abort the abnormal, and to euthanize the elderly. It is not so much love for those who suffer, but anger rooted in pride at the fact of suffering that provides the deepest motive power in the drive for societal change among Progressive faiths.

7. Salvation Comes Through Human Effort Alone

In Progressive belief, the salvation that comes through the radical reordering of the external world is brought about solely by human effort.

Christianity presents a radical solution to the problem of evil and a correspondingly complete transformation of the individual and of human society. Yet this salvation is accomplished by the initiative and power of God himself. Though God enlists the aid of humans in renewing the world, he does so in a manner that accomplishes the healing of the root moral problem of our alienation, namely

our pride. Hence Christians are faced with an often irritating but always salutary eschatological scheme: the perfect kingdom of God is "already, but not yet" established. The constant admonition given to those seeking salvation in Christ and the renewal of creation is to "wait on the Lord." Perseverance, trust, patient endurance, obedience, humility; these and virtues like them, by addressing the moral wound of pride, allow human participation in the world's healing and salvation, a process that is being accomplished in God's own time and God's own way, according to a schedule and a program that humans did not initiate and cannot control.

The Progressive believer is promised salvation not by waiting on God and learning the patient lessons of humility, but by seizing the means and the task of curing the world's ills by energetic action. Humanity has come of age; we are no longer children or slaves, and no longer under the cruel necessity of enduring life's hardships. Now is the time for the human race to rise up and grasp our destiny with our own hands. One can see why the Gnostic turn of mind is so tempting and crops up so often in the history of Christianity. It is not easy to wait on God for the solution to problems that we think we can fix for ourselves. Especially when we lose a keen sense of our own moral wounds, it is difficult to believe – with the wonders of modern science and the wealth of social and psychological learning we have been accumulating – that we do not have the ability to set the world right through our own efforts. Nominally Christian societies – places where the Christian vision of perfection and the hope of salvation have long been foundational for the society's life, but where faith, humility, and knowledge of personal sinfulness have waned – are ripe seed-beds for the growth of varieties of Gnostic belief systems that emphasize self-redemption rather than salvation by God in Christ.

8. The Application of a Technique (Gnosis) to Bring About Salvation

The Progressive method of accomplishing the re-ordering of the world is the application of a particular technical knowledge – gnosis – to the problems of existence.

For Progressive believers, "knowledge saves." Salvation is to be achieved, not by inner moral regeneration – there is no need for that – but by the application of a technique, whether spiritual, political, social/cultural, psychological, biological, technological, or maybe all of them at once, a technique that alters the world or our relationship to it and that undoes the evil that is alienating us. Hence the aptness of the term *gnostic* to describe Progressive salvific faiths. Applying knowledge to life's problems is not unique to Gnostic believers; it is what humans have always done. The defining note of a Gnostic scheme is the totality of the salvation believed to be brought about by technical power, a power that gives its holders control over the ways of the world and that places the initiative in bringing about a morally new world order in humanity's capable hands.

The rise of science in the early modern period had a thick slice of the neo-Gnostic attitude. Francis Bacon's often violent images concerning the way knowledge was to be wrested and seduced from the natural world to give greater power to humans was couched in Christian clothing – it was said to be part of the coming of the Kingdom of the Saints – but in Bacon's scheme the task of transforming the world was put squarely on the shoulders of enterprising men. Magic and science were pursued enthusiastically side by side during the early modern period; Isaac Newton was as interested in alchemy and the secret knowledge of the Kabbalah as he was in the natural laws of physics. Both science and magic were studied as paths for gaining the hidden technical knowledge that would save

the world. As things worked out, natural science proved the stronger magic; it got better results than alchemy and witchcraft. But the driving force behind the two developments was often similar: the search for a technique that would give us the power to save ourselves and set ourselves free. Doctor Faustus – the mythic evil genius of the modern period, whose academic degree was in theology – was both a scientist and a magician.

The explosive power of recent technologies and the development of intricate theories of social and psychological engineering have given Progressive believers' hopes of salvation a great boost. There is no necessary reason why technological and societal advances have to proceed according to a Gnostic set of assumptions, and for much of Western history such progress was not Gnostic in its aims. But the Gnostic strain is strong in the continuing modern quest for technical mastery. Like the magician, the modern technocrat is interested in power by whatever means possible. Part of the air we breathe, one of modernity's unacknowledged first principles, is the faith that technical scientific and social-scientific knowledge – often divorced from moral constraints – will save the world.

One result of the belief that radical personal and social transformation can be attained through the application of a particular technique is what might be called the "silver bullet" mentality. It is typical of Progressive programs for the betterment of the world that highly complex human problems are reduced to a single phenomenon that can be addressed and properly adjusted by the application of a particular technical solution. All will be well "if…". Progressive religion tends naturally to a world run by "experts," those special people who possess the silver bullet, the applied technique that will slay the evil in question and bring about the desired goal. This simplistic way of proceeding makes sense when servicing automobiles or air

conditioners. It runs into serious problems when the same mentality is applied to mysteriously complex matters of human psychology, social relations, and the immortal soul's quest for its eternal destiny.

9. A Dualistic View of History

Progressive religion proclaims a dualistic view of history and holds out a promise that the coming new age of freedom will decisively triumph over the past age of darkness and oppression.

Christians know that as long as humans suffer from the wound of sin, and as long as the world is under the influence of the devil, there can be no final victory over evil. Christians are full of hope, because the decisive battle against darkness has been won by Christ, and though the totality of that victory is still to come, they are already experiencing the beginnings of its fulfillment. But Christians also understand that the daily struggle against evil and the daily fight for goodness and justice are the necessary conditions of humanity in this age, important elements of a time during which God is testing and sifting human souls to make them worthy of their true home. No humanly devised formula, policy, or technique will enable us to dodge the necessity of that divinely ordained sifting process.

Progressive religion rejects this Christian attitude as negative and defeatist. Having once denied the reality of the Fall, the only reasonable goal for Progressive believers is a world substantially freed from evil. What emerges in every Progressive religious scheme is a dualistic vision of two completely different ages. By applying the requisite saving technique, the human race will escape from the age of *necessity*, an age of repression, darkness, alienation, and injustice in which virtually everything is bad, and will burst forth into the age of *freedom*, an age of light, harmony, justice, and peace in which nearly everything will be good. The break between the two ages is radical

and total, and it will result in a complete transformation of human life within the confines of time and history. Anything existing in the current age of oppression can be sacrificed or destroyed for the sake of the coming age of freedom.

An important dogma of modern Progressive faiths is the claim that we are now living in a unique time called the "modern age" (which in this context includes the notion of "post-modernity"), an age that is a qualitatively new era of history, in which traditional ways of thought and belief cannot be valid for our time by an inner necessity of the historical process. There are no universally valid truths, whether moral or rational, that apply both to the age of oppression and the age of freedom. Traditional values, traditional modes of rationality, and long-standing customs should not be consulted as a guide. In fact, because they have been part of the past oppressive age they probably need to be repudiated. Under the influence of this belief, the notion of dialogue – the interaction of two minds according to the dictates of rationality (*logos*) – loses its meaning, since there is no single rationality that spans the two ages. Progressive believers do not typically argue against traditional philosophies, beliefs, or moral norms on their own merits. They label them as outdated, oppressive, reactionary, or obscurantist, and therefore unworthy of serious consideration, needing to be shouted down or cancelled.

Here one can see again how Progressive religion receives the Christian vision and then alters it. Most ancient, tribal, and Eastern cultures have tended to a cyclic view of history, in which natural patterns and events repeat themselves rhythmically (again, "The Circle of Life"). In contrast, the Jewish (and thus Christian) sense is that things are moving toward a culmination, under the wisdom and providential care of God. Christianity teaches that the action of God makes all things new: *If anyone is in Christ, he is a new creation.*

The old is gone; behold, the new is come (2 Cor 5:17). Yet this promise of change and renewal is informed by Christ's insistence that he did not come to destroy the order of creation but to heal it of its corruptions and bring it to its true and intended state. The Old Covenant is not annihilated, as the second-century Gnostic heretic Marcion would have it, but is fulfilled and completed by the New. Therefore, the full coming of the kingdom of justice and goodness will not come about by merely human action in this age of the world. But the modern utopian takes this Christian sense for historical progression and fulfillment and impatiently sets aside any divine timetable or providence in favor of a new theory that makes Progress itself inevitable and noble, part of the very dynamic of the historical process. Logically, then, the past is inferior by a kind of necessity. Technical advances like refrigeration and social developments like sexual liberation can equally be expected to arise with all other good things from this dynamic, forward movement through time.[9] Belief in this pseudo-Christian theory of history gives the name "Progressive" to the faith we have been describing; this is what it means to be "on the right side of history."[10]

---

[9] Hegel's philosophy of history, a source for some of this thinking, attempts to discover a progressive direction and meaning in history, noting as an example that the world has progressed from one person being free (the pharaoh or emperor) to some persons being free (wealthy citizens) to all persons being free. Eric Voegelin, in *The New Science of Politics* (1952), referred to the utopian dream of progress as an attempt to "immanentize the eschaton."

[10] The *Catechism of the Catholic Church* poignantly teaches: *Before Christ's second coming the Church must pass through a final trial that will shake the faith of many believers. The persecution that accompanies her pilgrimage on earth will unveil the "mystery of iniquity" in the form of* ***a religious deception offering men an apparent solution to their problems at the price of apostasy from the truth.*** *The supreme religious deception is that of the Antichrist, a pseudo-messianism by which man glorifies himself in place of God and of his Messiah come in the flesh. The Antichrist's deception already begins to take shape in the world* ***every time the claim is made to realize within history that messianic hope which can only be realized beyond history through the eschatological judgment.*** *The Church has rejected even modified forms of this falsification of the kingdom to come under the name of millenarianism, especially the "intrinsically perverse" political form of a secular messianism* (§ 675-676, emphasis added).

The doctrine of the radical distinction between the two ages helps to explain the Progressive love for the mythic reconstruction of the past versus the present (and future) into a dualistic picture of good and evil. In order to give credibility to the Progressive doctrine of the two ages, the past – the supposed age of darkness and alienation – is painted in the bleakest colors possible. At the same time the horrors of the emerging age of freedom, especially when they come at the hands of Progressive agents, are overlooked or explained away. Thus the Progressive view of the Medieval period is insistently one of barbarism, ignorance, intolerance, and violence; nothing is too stupid or too cruel for the medievals, and the word itself is used as a negative epithet. Serious historians have known for generations that this view of the Middle Ages is nonsense, but this does not adjust the Progressive mindset, since belief in the darkness of the past is necessary for the success of the Progressive mythic picture. On the other hand, something as obvious as the horrors of Soviet communism were for many years ignored by Progressive believers and even now are too often downplayed or swept under the rug. Given Progressive assumptions, this is understandable: the past *had* to be horrible, and the post-revolutionary Progressive regime *had* to be liberating, not as observed facts, but as a matter of dogma.

The Progressive belief that the application of the right salvific practice will bring about an entirely new age of freedom, justice, and human flourishing is not the result of logic or scientific demonstration; it is a doctrine taken entirely on faith, and it should be noted that it is a very blind faith. Such a claim about the future obviously cannot be proven; but there is also a massive amount of evidence from failed Progressive religious projects that place the doctrine seriously in doubt. The tenacity with which the dogma is held, given that there is virtually no evidence in its favor and mountains of evidence

telling against it, points to a certain anti-rational and fundamentalistic quality of Progressive faiths. Despite the constant claim to be scientific, Progressive belief enlists scientific data only when that data supports previously embraced dogmatic theories. Whenever Progressive dogma collides with unfavorable scientific data, it is the data that gets ignored, suppressed, or shouted down, while the dogma is proclaimed as the ultimate reality.

10. Two Distinct Kinds of Humans

In a Progressive religious scheme, two distinct and antagonistic types of humans emerge: those who have embraced the new age of freedom, and those still tied to the old age of oppression.

The decisive change of the ages brought about by the Progressive transformation of the world also identifies two decisively different kinds of humans. Possession of the proper gnosis gives rise to a new type of person. Sometimes the knowledge involved is highly esoteric and intentionally restricted to a few, as was true of ancient Gnostic systems. Sometimes it is on offer for whoever might want it, as in many modern Progressive forms of faith, though even with these there lingers a strong sense of a "knowledge elite," of the few who really know and who can be trusted with power to arrange the new world, as against the many who are unenlightened and who should be content to follow them.

The division of the world into the enlightened and unenlightened helps explain much of the lack of consistency shown by those under the influence of Progressive religion in their behavior and attitudes toward the two opposed groups. According to the logic of its position, Progressive belief will naturally deal with those embracing the age of freedom – the "new humans," as the Communists often used to call them – in one way, and will treat those clinging to the age of

oppression in a very different way. The names of the two antagonistic groups change, but the underlying structure is similar. It may be the revolutionaries versus the reactionaries, the progressives against the obscurantists, the tolerant versus the hatemongers, the feminists against the sexists, the victimized against the privileged, the egalitarians versus the racists, or the greens versus the climate deniers. Enlightened believers can be trusted with power since they possess the requisite knowledge and proper beliefs and are therefore fundamentally good. The unenlightened cannot be trusted with power since they are participants in oppressive structures and are therefore fundamentally evil. The mistakes and foibles of the enlightened are bumps along the road and can be minimized or overlooked; similar crimes among the unenlightened are permanently unforgivable. Enlightened believers can be assumed to be basically well-meaning, honest, accurate, and impartial in their assessments, research, and reportage. Unenlightened non-believers are by necessity biased and tainted. The Progressive believer is thus tolerant toward the enlightened, but often brooks no tolerance whatever toward the unenlightened.

It is important to see that these categories are not the result of careful observation of data; they are doctrines taken on faith. Progressive believers have assumed that they are themselves unfallen and morally superior to their opponents, not by a careful examination of contrasting lives, nor by thinking themselves individually perfect or beyond critique – most Progressive believers do not think that – but as a religious doctrine that is held apart from evidence. Again, it is an article of Progressive faiths that they are on the "right side of history" and are "morally up-to-date," and that those who resist the doctrines of their faith are necessarily dark and bad. Progressive believers are therefore "nice" while their opponents are "nasty" or "scary." Progressives are the peace-lovers, the friendly people, the

generous and reasonable ones. If the data happen to show in a given instance that this is not the case, it will do nothing to alter the viewpoint. It *has* to be true; it is an article of Progressive faith.

The Progressive division of the world into absolute categories of good and evil people corresponds to and borrows from the Christian division of the world into the (ultimately) saved and damned. But in the Christian understanding, good and evil cannot be mapped decisively onto discrete groups of people in this age of the world; the line that divides good from evil runs through every human heart and is found both inside and outside the Church. Further, the final division of the human race will not definitively happen until the end of the ages, a responsibility that belongs solely to an all-knowing and all-just God. Until that time, for Christians it is impossible to know with certainty who might end up on one or the other side of the line. Hence Saint Paul's admonition to the Corinthians: *"Do not pronounce judgment before the time, before the Lord comes, who will bring to light the things now hidden in darkness and will disclose the purposes of the heart"* (1 Cor 4:5). It is also the case that Christians understand their primary opponents to be not other humans but non-human, demonic powers. Christianity urges its followers genuinely to love their (human) enemies and hope for their rescue, and to reserve their hatred for the evil spirits who oppress the world.

Progressive religion, on the other hand, claims to be able to divide the human race between the good and the evil *in the present*, and it places the authority to make such judgments in the hands of other (enlightened) humans. And since Progressive religion denies the existence of evil spirits, it becomes necessary to demonize whole segments of the human race who are then marginalized and, if necessary, eradicated for the health and salvation of the world.

Given these beliefs concerning the chasm between the age of freedom and the age of oppression, and between the enlightened and the unenlightened, it can be seen why it is all-important for Progressive believers to identify themselves and others as members of the new humanity, since there is so much at stake in the identification. Modes of dress, manners of speech, use of symbols, communal expressions of religious belief, patterns of diet, books and news sources, bumper stickers and yard signs, and even opinions about otherwise trivial matters all take on an importance entirely out of proportion to their intrinsic significance. Communities of like-minded believers are sought out and protected. Much of the tendency toward what is sometimes characterized as "virtue signaling" arises due to the understandable need among Progressive believers to identify themselves with the saved and separate themselves from the damned. Despite much rhetoric about diversity to the contrary, Progressive religious enclaves tend to be highly monocultural and homogeneous (think of certain Brooklyn or San Francisco neighborhoods, or almost any university faculty), tightly monitored communities that resist contact with non-believers and run them out of town when they find them. Yet such inconsistencies are understandable in light of Progressive religious assumptions.

11. Revolution as the Process by which Salvation is Achieved

Revolution – the annihilation of the structures of oppression – is the privileged means by which Progressive belief will bring about the new age of freedom.

A momentous aspect of Progressive religion is its view of revolution. This is clear in Karl Marx's famous revolutionary dictum, "The philosophers have hitherto only interpreted the world in various

ways. The point, however, is to change it."[11] Through most of history, especially among those who have held to a perennial view of rationality and morality, "revolution" has not been a very positive word or idea. Violent revolution, whether political, social, or cultural, might be necessary as a desperate remedy in a given case, but it is like performing an invasive operation on a human body: it should be avoided if possible, since it tends to weaken the constitution of the patient and might prove fatal. More to the point for Christians has been "reform," the constant and usually more gradual process of re-aligning the patterns of personal and social life to perennial moral and spiritual realities, an activity that can often be unsettling but that tends to purify and re-vivify rather than destroy. Progressive faiths view the idea of revolution differently and far more positively. In Progressive belief, revolution is salvific: it is the act of overthrowing and annihilating the oppressive structures of the current evil order and setting the stage for an entirely new and liberated order, a transformation that will necessarily and spontaneously take place once the old order has been destroyed. This again requires a strong act of faith, since there is little evidence that such revolutions have ever produced the hoped-for results. The contrary is more evident, that neo-Gnostic revolutions have generally left things in far worse shape than they had been before. Nonetheless, the belief in the sacredness and efficacy of revolution remains the mainspring of Progressive action and the source of much of its attractive power: the confident hope in a glorious future state that will come about – no one quite knows how – by the complete destruction of what currently exists.

This attitude toward revolution motivated the French Jacobins in their readiness to destroy old institutions and to declare 1792

---

11 *Theses on Feuerbach*

"the Year 1." It underlay Marx's claim that the state would "wither away" after the proletarian revolution. It informed the "Burn Baby Burn" slogan of 60's radical activists and gave chic and the halo of martyrdom to Che Guevara. It provides the confidence of feminists, queer theorists, sexual liberationists, and black power proponents that the destruction of patriarchy, heteronormativity, white privilege, and traditional ideas about marriage and sex will automatically bring about a new era of happiness and freedom.

In Progressive religion, violence is thus not an accidental event or an unfortunate corruption of high ideals. When applied to the annihilation of the perceived structures of oppression, violence is a morally good activity, a positive and praiseworthy act. Given this doctrine, it should come as no surprise that believers of Progressive faiths have been the most violent people the world has ever produced, if the number of millions of people killed is taken as the measure. Progressive religion regularly turns to systematic violence, not because its adherents are specially nasty people – though some of them have been – but by the demands of its own inner logic.

Belief in the need for revolutionary change to escape oppression and gain freedom explains the emergence of the "cancel culture" currently so rife among Progressive believers. It is not enough to improve things; it is not sufficient to view the world as a place where good and evil are inevitably present, and to promote the good even while recognizing that a certain amount of evil will accompany everything fallen humans attempt. The age of oppression needs to be blotted out and denied existence entirely, lest it continue to taint the age of freedom. This program of willful systematic amnesia begins with artifacts – statues, texts, uses of language – but if the requisite power is gained it always moves on to eliminating living humans. The logic of tearing down statues and erasing words is the same as

the impetus behind the French Revolutionary Reign of Terror, the Soviet gulag, the Chinese cultural revolution, and the Nazi death camps. The sources and expressions of evil must be hunted down and eliminated so that the pure society can properly arrive.

In a given Progressive religious scheme, the revolution – the change from repression to liberation – may be conceived as sharp and decisive, or it may be formulated as a more gradual process. Each revolutionary path has had its examples and proponents. In either case, what is accomplished is a complete break with and destruction of the old; the only question is whether the change is short and sharp, as in the French, Russian, Nazi, and Chinese revolutions, or longer and more gradual, as in the scientistic positivist revolution articulated by Comte, or the revolution of spirit outlined by Hegel, or the psychological revolution promoted by the followers of Freud, or the Euro-communist transformation of societal institutions promoted by Antonio Gramsci.

Gradualist methods often arise among Progressive believers in a humane attempt to soften the violent edges of revolution, born of revulsion at the barbarities perpetrated by revolutionaries and the hostile reactionary momentum they often produce. But there seems to be a lingering conviction within Progressive communities of faith that the radical revolutionaries are the real believers. Politically motivated lesbians are the true feminists; Che and the Marxist guerillas are the real leftist political heroes; rioters and cop killers are the genuine battlers for civil rights; transgender activists are the front-line fighters for sexual liberation. A sense of ideological inferiority experienced by those who prefer a gradual process to more decisive and often violent action can be detected in the reluctance shown by advocates of peaceful revolution to condemn violent revolutionaries. They seem to be secretly in sympathy with their bloodier and more conflictive

comrades and appear to envy their boldness and their results. This attitude has been observable among many Progressive believers in the academic community and in the political world. Though often professing peaceful means of change and maybe even preferring such means, they find themselves unable to condemn acts of coercion and violence that they themselves might not be likely to commit.

The revolutionary dogma at the heart of Progressive religion finds a certain resonance in human nature. It is rooted in our awareness that evil must be battled as a matter of conscience and that something must die if the guilty human race is to be purified. This instinct is as old as humanity and can be found in every human culture. When it has taken a dark turn it has given rise to the practice of human sacrifice. More benign expressions can be seen in the nearly universal practice of offering sacrifices of animals and food to the gods. In Christianity those foreshadowings found their fulfillment in an act of overwhelming mercy: the extraordinary sacrifice of Christ on the Cross. It turned out that blood did indeed have to be shed, and that someone did need to die if humanity was to be set free of guilt, and that someone was God himself. With the neo-Gnostic denial of the Fall, the instinct for sacrifice and blood-letting has not disappeared, but it has turned outward, away from the mitigation of personal guilt toward the elimination of the demonized non-believer.

Like the Christianity out of which it has grown, the many variants of Progressive religion are highly evangelistic. Unlike Christianity, in attempting to gain adherents to their cause, the preferred strategy – one would almost say the necessary strategy – is to foment anger. Most people are not easily moved to engage in conflict, and yet conflict – revolutionary action against evil structures – is the only means by which Progressive salvation can arrive. How is this reluctance to be overcome, and how are people to be energized for

the cause of freedom? The most effective way has been to inflame their anger, their resentment, and their fear – a process sometimes called "consciousness-raising" – so that they will be ready to pursue revolutionary violence against oppressive structures. Anger – "rage," as it is usually termed in this context – will beget the destruction that will lead to all good things.

It is one of the many incongruities of Progressive religion that it claims to be productive of peace, attributing the social turmoil and violence it engenders to its opponents, when in fact rage and resentment against perceived enemies are the necessary atmosphere for its success, without which it dies. The life and soul of Progressive religious practice involves stoking anger for the fight against those who are inhibiting the birth of the age of freedom. If such enemies are not obviously forthcoming, Progressive believers need to invent them, lest their mythic picture of the world should dissolve. Counter-revolutionaries, enemies of the people, reactionary elements, Jews and Jew-lovers, bearers of white privilege, sexists, racists, haters, bigots, pigs: the historic list of necessary enemies is long and gets ever longer.

It is in the nature of neo-Gnostic belief systems that they operate within other belief structures, at least for a time, and many of those who have assumed Progressive dogmas do not hold those beliefs in their entirety or with consistency. For many, perhaps for most, the beliefs and dogmas outlined above are often hidden away, held in muted form, and act as unexamined first principles that only partially dominate ideas about what is true and how things ought to work. But such hidden principles tend to become more explicit and to be applied with increasing consistency over time.

12. The Necessary Failure of Modern Religion

The Progressive revolution always ultimately fails, because Progressive belief is founded on a radical departure from reality. Paradoxically, the more completely a given revolution succeeds, the more complete will be its resulting failure.

Faith in the positive effects of revolutionary destruction and confidence in the birth of a new age of liberation rising from the ashes of the old order is perhaps the greatest illusion in every neo-Gnostic Progressive scheme. Yet because they are founded on erroneous views of God, the world, and humanity, Progressive faiths always fail in bringing about their promised liberation.[12] Not only are they incapable of effecting serious improvement, but by destroying much of the institutional and cultural fabric necessary for any reasonably happy and sane human life, such revolutions leave desolate human wastelands behind them.

For this reason, Progressive religion is most attractive and most potent before the hoped-for revolution has occurred or while it is still happening. Progressive believers can point to obvious and egregious evils in the existing world, and they can instill a hope of overcoming those evils in the future. All this is highly compelling; it appeals to both the good human desire to confront evil and the bad human tendency to deny personal guilt and to seek an external source of the world's ills. This combined appeal can be difficult to resist, especially for the young who have little experience of themselves or the world. If Progressive religion were able to maintain itself forever in a pre-revolutionary phase of hopeful anticipation, its attractiveness might be sustained. But the greatest blow to Progressive faith occurs

---

12 They are what Patrick Deneen, author of *Why Liberalism Failed*, in a 2019 lecture at the University of Mary, described as "ideologies": philosophies of human life that are inadequate to the human person, that do not map onto human nature.

when the revolution succeeds. Progressive believers then take hold of the power they have sought to usher in the new age, when the time has come for the fulfillment of their bright promises. Due to the impossibility of making good on those promises, the hoped-for paradise never arrives.

What Happens When the Revolution Inevitably Fails

When the paradise promised by a Progressive faith, whatever its specific contours, is not forthcoming despite significant revolutionary activity, and when life seems to be getting worse rather than better, a crisis occurs in the Progressive mind. During the first stage of the crisis, the grim consequences of failed revolution are ignored or shouted down, and a spirit of mendacity gains influence. The claim is made that the revolution has not gone far enough, or that there are counter-revolutionaries who are betraying the cause, or that the revolution has really made everyone very happy. During this stage, anyone who dares to point out the revolution's failure is bullied and marginalized and, if necessary, silenced and done away with. Such was the propaganda machine that operated for many decades in Soviet Russia and for a shorter time in Nazi Germany. Such is the spirit of modern Progressive believers toward those who point out the harmful effects of the sexual revolution or the drawbacks of unnuanced multiculturalism or radical feminism. The growth of this culture of lies is unfortunate but inevitable. To admit that the revolution did not bring about the desired change would be to abandon the Progressive faith, and with it all hope for a better world.

At a certain point a second stage in the crisis is reached, when the weight of dismal reality can no longer be supported and the revolu-

tion in question is increasingly discredited. The constant propaganda grows ever more hollow in the wake of the human suffering brought about by Progressive utopian illusions. The difficult fact then has to be faced, if not by the revolution's leaders whose access to power is at stake, then by many of its adherents and fellow travelers, that the revolution has substantially failed. This recognition of revolutionary failure gives rise to three main responses among different people, and sometimes in the same person at different times.

(1) A first response is simple disillusionment. Many of those whose hopes have been so sadly disappointed by the false dogmas of their failed religion fall into cynicism and despair. They cease to think that there is any way out of the human predicament, and they lapse into some mode of coping with their despair: pleasure-seeking, incessant media distraction, workaholism, substance addiction, or suicide. If the experience of disillusion takes a philosophic form, it expresses itself in a form of nihilism – the conviction that existence has no meaning. After each failed Progressive revolution of the modern period, one could trace the predictable arrival of nihilistic philosophy: the French revolution, then disillusionment at its failure, then Nietzsche; the Bolshevik revolution, then despair at its corruption, then Camus, Sartre, and proponents of Critical Theory.

(2) A second response seems the most common among serious Progressive believers. For many who are faced with a failed revolution, the specific form of Progressive salvation that has been discredited is quietly set aside, while the deep structure of belief is maintained. Rather than abandon the faith altogether, these believers will seek another expression of Progressive faith and sign up for a different, perhaps deeper kind of revolution that promises to get the job done

better. Something like this has taken place in much of the assessment of both the Soviet and Nazi revolutions of the last century. Few would now simply defend those attempts to remake the world, but for many, the first principles behind the movements have not been repudiated, only reformulated in a different guise and with greater nuance. It is a pattern that regularly takes place. It is therefore not surprising to find East German Fascists becoming exemplary Communists in the postwar Eastern Block of Europe, or youthful Woodstock revolutionaries of the 1960s effortlessly transforming themselves into the magnates of the Silicon Valley electronic revolution, or former Polish Communists so quickly embracing progressive technocratic capitalism, or (privileged white) feminists joining rioters against privileged whites. In each case there is a similar underlying salvific structure to the movements and a corresponding promise of radical human transformation. The shift from one religious expression to another is a shorter road to travel than it may seem from outward appearances.

(3) A third response is the most hopeful from a Christian point of view. Revolutionary failure can produce a serious re-evaluation of the underlying structure of Progressive belief and provoke a desire to find a completely different way forward. If the re-evaluation results in repentance from pride and a readiness to put aside the tempting but vain hope of gaining freedom from alienation by human efforts alone and a readiness to seek help from God, an opening is made for the embrace of a more genuine faith. Christian renewal has always been spurred by failed utopian revolutions. There have been religious revivals following the French revolution, the Nazi defeat, and the collapse of the Soviet Union.

It may help at this point to summarize those aspects of modern Progressive religion that make it so captivating to many people, and especially to the young. The religion of the day can sometimes be dismissed, especially in its more advanced and extreme expressions, as obviously untrue, destructive, or unworkable, and therefore hardly worth serious consideration. Yet despite its lacks, there is much about it that moves the human mind and spirit. Consider: here is a religion that (1) issues a high and compelling moral call; (2) promises to overcome the aching sense of not fitting into the world; (3) looks toward a glorious future of increasing perfection; (4) has an adventurous edge and issues a decisive call to action; (5) appeals to the inventive capacity of the human mind to solve problems and to improve existence; (6) absolves the believer of personal guilt; and (7) echoes the truths of Christianity in ways that appeal to our created nature and respond to certain desires given us by God. Like many deceptive or problematic things, its darker side is not immediately apparent and often becomes clear only over time. A good understanding of the attractiveness of Progressive religion is a necessary first step in countering its influence, whether in the wider society or in our own lives.

III

Some Further Notes on Progressive, Neo-Gnostic Religion

HAVING TOUCHED UPON the structure and qualities of modern, Progressive religion, let us now briefly examine some of its deeper roots. Doing so will help to clarify, later, some of the contours of the apostolic stance we will want to take up in our engagement with it, as well as some of the reasons why we must learn to engage it also in its subtler appearances.

1. The Gnostic Outlook Through History

In one form or another, Gnostic belief systems have been a constant antagonist to Christianity from its beginnings, arising partly from Christian ideas and partly from elements foreign to Christianity. Gnostic tendencies were attacked in the pages of the New Testament, and Gnostic teachers like Simon Magus and Marcion were among the early Church's first opponents. Second-century Christian apologists such as Saint Irenaeus, Saint Justin Martyr, and Tertullian viewed Gnosticism as the greatest threat facing the Church's life. In the fourth century, Saint Augustine adhered for many years to the Gnostic sect of the Manichaeans before he turned to Christianity, a sign of the attractiveness of the Gnostic attitude even for gifted minds. In the fifth century, Pope Saint Leo the Great often explicitly

preached against Gnosticism. In the eleventh century, Joachim of Fiore articulated an influential theory of history with strong Gnostic elements. In the twelfth and thirteenth centuries, the Albigensians, whom Saint Dominic sought to win back to orthodox belief, held a form of Gnostic faith, and the Franciscan movement was troubled by splinter groups with strong Gnostic tendencies like the Fraticelli. Saint Thomas Aquinas marshaled many arguments against the Gnostic errors of his day; Thomist philosopher Josef Pieper called Gnosticism Aquinas's constant and primary adversary. [13] The Protestant Reformation gave an opening to certain religious sects and currents of thought with Gnostic propensities, especially those associated with the more radical forms of Puritanism, currents that are still alive in some modern expressions of Protestantism. Gnostic attitudes can be seen in the development of modern "theologies of liberation" that have emerged mainly in Catholic settings. And as we have been noting, a good deal of what goes loosely by the name of progressive or liberal Christianity is fundamentally Gnostic in its structure.

Though clothed in diverse garments at different times, the principles that underlie the Gnostic attitude are similar in every age. The two qualities that usually come to mind in discussing ancient Gnosticism are a deprecation of all things material and the acquisition of highly esoteric and hidden knowledge known only to a few initiates. For those of the broader Gnostic turn of mind, however, these qualities are possible but not necessary responses to yet deeper principles about the nature of the universe. It is possible to hold a Gnostic view of reality that is not obviously characterized by either of these aspects, or at least that does not put them at the center of

---

13 *The Four Cardinal Virtues*

its system. And while it is possible to trace historical connections between different Gnostic groups through the centuries, Gnostic believers of one age have not usually been dependent upon those of a previous age for their beliefs and ideas. The Gnostic attitude does not depend on passing on a tradition after the manner of Judaism or Christianity; it arises of itself out of the soil of Christian belief. Even where connections are made by contemporary Gnostics with those of former times, it seems more a recognition of affinity of thought than an acknowledgement of a source for their own ideas. The consistent presence of this dark shadow upon the Christian faith can be understood as the inevitable development that comes about whenever Christians grow collectively proud.

Much Enlightenment and post-Enlightenment thought can be characterized as variants of the Gnostic attitude as it grew out of Christianity. Such elements can be traced in the Baconian vision of science and in many of its leading practitioners, such as Isaac Newton and Robert Boyle. Neo-Gnostic attitudes are paramount in the political philosophy of Rousseau and of the Jacobins of the French Revolution. G. F. W. Hegel articulated a philosophy with strong Gnostic tendencies, one that Karl Marx reworked into a powerful expression of revolutionary religion. Fascism, and especially Nazism, had a fundamentally Gnostic structure. The neo-Gnostic religious stance can be discerned as the deep structure of many modern movements that appear at first sight to be different from and sometimes even opposed to each other, from radical feminism to movements for black empowerment, to the sexual liberation movement, to currents within the green movement, to transhumanism.

Just as there have been conflicts and wars of religion between variants of the Christian faith which have held a similar overall view of the world, so there are and have been conflicts and even

wars between variants of neo-Gnostic religion. The source of the conflict in both cases is similar: the warring parties are fighting over the same piece of religious turf. To take one example: Nazism and Soviet Communism were both neo-Gnostic belief systems, and as such were profoundly indebted to and at the same time deeply hostile to the Greek-Christian culture and religious world that preceded them. They were also mortal enemies of each other. The antagonism between leftist "progressives" and rightist "reactionaries" has been the main identity trope of modern intellectuals for the past century. Leftist neo-Gnostics, who have dominated the conversation, like to situate Fascist neo-Gnostics as their extreme opposites at the other end of the spectrum of ideas and to brand anyone who dissents from their orthodoxy a Fascist. But despite certain theoretical differences between Fascism and Communism, the two are blood brothers founded on similar first principles, as can be seen by the outcome of their ideas whenever they are put into practice. It is not accidental that Mussolini, the founder of modern Fascism, was a disciple of the Bolshevik Lenin. These two expressions of modern religion were so hostile to each other partly because they were fighting to dominate the same revolutionary ground.[14]

A similar battle is currently brewing between radical feminists and the proponents of the "trans" movement. For unavoidable reasons, these two expressions of revolutionary faith are on a collision course. But despite their conflict, they are rooted in similar first principles. They are both expressions of a neo-Gnostic form of self-salvation.

---

14 This from Roger Scruton, in *Fools, Frauds, and Firebrands* (2015): *It is a testimony to the success of communist propaganda that it has been able to persuade so many people that fascism and communism are polar opposites and that there is a single scale of political ideology stretching from 'far left' to 'far right.'... It is perhaps easier for an English writer than it is for an Italian to see through that nonsense, and to perceive what it is designed to conceal: the deep structural similarity between communism and fascism, both as theory and as practice.*

2. The Derivative Nature of Gnostic Faiths

There is a special difficulty that arises in attempting to identify neo-Gnostic religion. Gnostic belief does not resolve itself into one consistent set of practices or institutional arrangements. It is rather a stance, a way of thinking, or (for many under the influence of its more romantic strains) even a mood, founded on key first principles but expressing those principles in many different ways. As a result, Gnosticism is inherently parasitic like a virus, or to put it more neutrally, it is derivative rather than original. The Gnostic turn of mind will inhabit an already existing religious faith or philosophic system and re-order the structure of its host body even while assuming that host's mythic power. Much of the potency of a given Gnostic belief system comes from what it has borrowed from an existing and internally more coherent way of seeing things. It is doubtful whether something called "pure Gnosticism" could exist for very long on its own; it is certain that it could not be an enduring influential force. There has never been a successful civilization founded on a Gnostic form of religion, and it is unlikely that there could be, given that many elements of Gnostic belief militate against any stable civilizational development. Thus, in speaking of Gnostic religion, one is not so much identifying a clear set of practices and institutional arrangements that remain constant over time as pointing to underlying first principles and dogmatic commitments that unite apparently disparate movements and ideologies.

The inherently derivative nature of the Gnostic attitude means that an existing religious system can be moved in a Gnostic direction to a greater or lesser degree. It is not a question of all or nothing, as it would be, for instance, in the case of a Christian becoming a Muslim or vice versa. In a given instance there might be present a slight Gnostic influence or a very strong one. Because those who

embrace a Gnostic attitude do so from within the context of an already existing religion or philosophy, they will continue to use the terms and categories of the host system until a growing lack of coherence causes disruption and it becomes necessary to explicitly renounce the host faith. Words, institutional offices, concepts, and narratives are given new meanings but are left superficially in their original form. Like wood that is slowly undergoing a process of petrification, the original shape, texture, and contours remain even as the fundamental substance is being changed. As a result, many of those under a strong neo-Gnostic influence do not easily perceive the fact. This amorphous nature of Gnosticism explains something of the Church's constant vigilance against various forms of Gnosticism throughout its history. Gnostic ideas do not usually begin as an external assault upon Christianity, though they often end there. First, they take root subtly within the Church and claim to offer the true meaning of the Christian faith even as they are subverting its foundations. Saint Irenaeus, the second-century theologian who wrote against Gnosticism, noted: "They talk like us, though thinking very differently."[15] The whole tenor of his work *Against Heresies* is one of unmasking and bringing to light a hidden but dangerous foe. The same has been true in every age.

Because Gnostic religion is derivative of other belief systems, and because there are inherent contradictions involved in Gnostic first principles, it becomes a futile task to look for logical consistency in a Gnostic worldview. In such an unstable alloy, there will be remaining bits from the host vision that do not square well with new Gnostic ideas. Variants of Gnostic religion tend to present a constantly shifting ground since their disparate elements cannot

---

15 *Against Heresies*

ultimately be reconciled. To repeat an important point, it is doubtful that it would be possible to construct a completely coherent Gnostic scheme, entirely divorced from assumptions gained from a host religion or philosophy. Marxist communism, the most thoroughgoing attempt at doing so, was still dependent for much of its attractive power on the Judeo-Christian faith that preceded it, and it has proved an incoherent and destructive failure whenever it has been put into practice. Modern neo-Gnostic beliefs have grown up in the context of Christianity, and current Gnostic movements are dependent to a great degree on the Christian vision of reality. It may not be intrinsic to Gnosticism that it needs to arise out of Christianity; ancient Gnosticism depended on Greek religion and philosophy for much of its narrative structure, and there were Gnostic elements in some strands of intertestamental Judaism. Certain modern Islamic sects seem to have as much in common with neo-Gnostic movements as with traditional Islam. But the modern Progressive religion that we face in the West is necessarily a post-Christian phenomenon; it has borrowed profoundly from Christianity, and its existence is unthinkable without the Jewish and Christian religion that preceded it. That is why we have paid special attention to the correspondences and divergences between Christianity and the neo-Gnostic faiths that have grown out of it and subverted it.

3. Politics and Modern Progressive Religion

Given our highly politicized world, it is inevitable that after a description of modern religion like the one given above, certain political questions will arise. How does neo-Gnostic religion map onto the current political landscape? Is this just a different way of characterizing leftist liberal politics? Does using the word "progressive" to describe modern religion simply attach it to the political parties that

have embraced that adjective for themselves? Are there neo-Gnostic expressions of faith on the "right" as well as on the "left"? Without attempting a thorough response to such questions, a task that would take us beyond the goal of this essay, some initial responses can be suggested that would repay further elaboration and nuance elsewhere.

First, a word concerning religion and politics. It has been an American tradition to say that politics and religion do not mix: politics is one thing, religion is another, and the two should keep separate from each other. The truth is that even in America religion and politics have always been intertwined in important ways. The American founders were not attempting to do away with religion; what they wanted to avoid was a confessional state. Even the non-believers among them considered religion a useful means of engendering moral virtue in the populace, without which none of them thought a democratic form of government could long survive. In any case, the only kind of religion that could entirely avoid influencing public life would hardly be worthy of the name of religion. It would be an entirely privatized personal hobby and could have nothing important to say to the world. Still, it has been generally true that American political leaders have been respectful of religious institutions and content to express their political authority mainly in temporal matters, leaving the moral and spiritual life of the citizen largely to the care of family and church. This acknowledgment of governmental limits was founded on a long tradition.

But it is often forgotten that it has not been typical for humanity to make a distinction between the spiritual and temporal authorities of a society. Most of the world's civilizations and cultures have lodged spiritual, moral, and political authority in the same office. Priestly kingship in some form has been the overwhelmingly favored type of human government through the ages. This makes a certain sense:

human life is a single integrated thing, and there is a simplicity and completeness in providing one authority to cover the whole of life. Jesus changed all that. With his striking judgment, *"Give to Caesar what is Caesar's, and to God what is God's"* (Mt 22:21), he taught that the secular authority was legitimate but not total, that it did not extend to the inner life of the soul. In Christian civilizations it has thus been held that there are two distinct authorities governing human life, a spiritual authority and a temporal authority. It has been recognized, if not always practiced, that the state should not be subject in strictly temporal matters to spiritual authorities, and that the church should not be relegated to a mere department of state. This dual set of authorities has historically been the source of a good bit of friction through the centuries, but it has been a genuine example of "creative tension." Our tradition of civil liberty and the practice of limited government can largely be traced to this dual source of authority. For Christians, therefore, the political aspect of life is important, but not ultimate.

We should expect that as our society increasingly distances itself from its Christian roots, the Christian sensibility for limited government will wane, and the universal human tendency to unite all authority, spiritual and temporal, in one central office or structure will reassert itself. This development has been progressing in fits and starts all over the Western world since the French Revolution. Once a Christian vision of the world has been abandoned, it is very difficult to limit the power of temporal governments. Given the fact that modern Progressive religion is overwhelmingly this-worldly in its scope, the political arena has increasingly become the staging ground for religious propagation and (often enough) for a kind of religious warfare, though its participants persist in denying the religious nature of their political visions.

What about the political "left" and "right"? Is neo-Gnostic religion simply to be identified with leftist politics? The first response to that question is to repeat what has often been observed: that the labels "left" and "right" – which first appeared during the French Revolution, when members of the National Assembly divided into supporters of the revolution and supporters of the *Ancien Régime* – have long since ceased to be helpful as descriptors. Stalinist communism and Nazi fascism were both forms of modern neo-Gnostic faith and, despite attempts to make them appear as opposites, they were in fact very close in their fundamental structure. The religious alternative to both of them is Christianity. Where genuinely Christian ideas predominate, neo-Gnostic religion loses influence.

During the nineteenth into the twentieth century in Europe, neo-Gnostic revolutionary religious movements flourished on both the "left" and the "right" of the political spectrum. Karl Marx and Friederich Engels began their famous Manifesto with the line: "A spectre is haunting Europe – the spectre of communism."[16] Socialistic communism, a force that emerged as a serious political power with the Russian Revolution of 1917, defined the phenomenon on the left. On the right, at the same time, there were simmering revolutionary movements across Europe in the guise of messianic religious nationalism. These two variants of gnostic faith eventually ran afoul of each other in World War II, which was, among other things, an internecine gnostic religious war between German Nazis and Russian Communists. Each of these ideologies was attempting to replace a waning Christianity with a new, all-encompassing vision for the society that promised the perfection of the temporal world.

---

16 *Communist Manifesto,* ch. 1

Unlike Europe, the United States has not until recentl strong political tradition of either fascist or communist neo-G faith. Throughout the twentieth century, the "right" in America was close to the nineteenth-century English liberal tradition, tending to promote freedom of markets and to favor less, rather than more, governmental regulation. The American "left" espoused a greater role of government in addressing social and economic questions. From a moral point of view, there was a loose general agreement around traditional values centered in the Ten Commandments. That older America, one that still haunts the memories of the two political parties, has been changing rapidly since the 1960s.

It could be argued that in the current American political environment, one of our major parties has more fully embraced a neo-Gnostic Progressive faith as its political platform while the other has maintained more elements from the tradition of limited government as it arose from Christian ideas. It therefore makes sense that serious Christians might increasingly support the one and increasingly leave the other. Yet the tendency for the pre-Christian tradition of limited temporal government to gather to itself all authority, moral and spiritual as well as temporal, is working its way on all political fronts. A subtle temptation therefore lurks for Christians even as they dutifully fulfill their obligations as citizens. Because Progressive religion expresses its hope to change the world entirely in the political arena, Christians can be influenced to think that politics is the primary activity of humanity. They can imitate the neo-Gnostic temptation to tie their foundational hopes to a particular political ideal and their loyalties to a political figure or a transitory political party, such that elections become events of epic importance. They can forget that our most significant battleground is not the political or legislative landscape but the individual human soul; that our ultimate enemy

is not a political party but a powerful spiritual being; and that the only way to establish the kingdom of God is by weapons of warfare suited to a spiritual battle.

4. A Special Case: The Rise and Dominance of the Therapeutic

In 2005, sociologists Christian Smith and Melina Lundquist Denton wrote a book called *Soul Searching: The Religious and Spiritual Lives of American Teenagers*, in which they identified the predominant beliefs of American teenagers. They famously coined the term "Moralistic Therapeutic Deism" or "MTD" to describe what those teenagers, including Christian ones, most commonly believed. They summed up the belief system in five core tenets:

1. A God exists who created and ordered the world and watches over human life on earth.
2. God wants people to be good, nice, and fair to each other, as taught in the Bible and by most world religions.
3. The central goal of life is to be happy and to feel good about oneself.
4. God does not need to be particularly involved in one's life except when God is needed to resolve a problem.
5. Good people go to heaven when they die.

This insightful formulation has rightly gained a lot of attention, since it quickly became obvious that MTD was not just the belief of millennial teenagers but was characteristic of whole swaths of the Christian world. In the context of our discussion here, the question arises whether MTD, an obviously widespread set of beliefs, is a form of neo-Gnostic faith. Our answer would be that in itself, it is not, but that it represents a degenerate and flaccid state of Christianity that is highly vulnerable to the preaching of a more potent and virulent

neo-Gnostic faith. If twenty years ago MTD was the closest thing to an American civil religion, it has been rapidly turning into something different and more dangerous, namely the Progressive religion we have been describing. Why is MTD so prone to the embrace of neo-Gnostic beliefs?

For two main reasons.

First, given the highly fragile state of personal identity so endemic to denizens of the modern world, people face a heightened level of psychic suffering. The universal experience of alienation has been magnified and made more excruciating by modern social conditions. Traditionally, humans have looked for ways to escape the inevitability of death, the burden of personal guilt, and the often-painful circumstances of physical existence. Moderns are generally more comfortable physically, but we suffer far more than our forebears did from loneliness, depression, and self-doubt. In such circumstances, the therapeutic concern to "feel good about oneself" gains a great deal of potency. When a faith comes along that promises entire freedom from alienation, those who have been grappling with their own inner psychic pain will find it to be particularly alluring.

Second, MTD orients its believers toward happiness in the present world. MTD does not explicitly deny the existence of God or of heavenly reality, but nearly all of its attention is focused on a person's experience of this current life. Such a way of thinking easily accommodates itself to a more potent neo-Gnostic faith that implicitly or explicitly denies the importance of God. Many Christians who fall into the vague Christian half-life of MTD – which at its best is a beige and uninteresting way to look at the world, a kind of Christianity Lite – may easily experience the allure of embracing a more demanding and heroic-seeming faith, readily found in variants of

Progressive religion. This is especially true among the young, whose sense of life's adventure has not yet been dulled.

IV

Catching All the Diseases of the World

"What the soul is to the body, Christians are to the world… The soul is enclosed in the body, but it holds the body together; and though Christians are detained in the world as if in a prison, they in fact hold the world together."

— Letter to Diognetus

"In this wicked world, in these evil days, when the Church measures her future loftiness by her present humility, and is exercised by goading fears, tormenting sorrows, disquieting labors, and dangerous temptations, when she soberly rejoices, rejoicing only in hope, there are many reprobates mingled with the good, and both are gathered together by the Gospel as in a drag net; and in this world, as in a sea, both swim enclosed without distinction in the net, until it is brought ashore, when the wicked must be separated from the good."

— Saint Augustine of Hippo[17]

1. The Holy Catholic Church?

CHRIST CAME AS A LIGHT into the darkness of a fallen world, and the darkness cannot put out that light. Our aim in looking into the specific nature of the darkness we are now facing is not to be

[17] *City of God,* book 18

overwhelmed by it, but rather to be better able to stand with Christ as he continues his work of saving the human race. Jesus founded the Church as a "rock," and promised that hell's gates would not prevail against it, and that he would be with his people to the end of the ages. The Church is the special instrument of God's action on earth, inhabited by the Holy Spirit, and gifted with the strength and resources to throw back whatever darkness the powers of evil may concoct.

Yet a question arises as we try to make sense of the Church's way through the world. Whenever a claim is made about the Church as the vehicle of Christ's presence on earth, an objection comes immediately to mind: if the Church is the dwelling place of God, if it is called by Jesus the *"light of the world"* (Mt 5:14), why is there so much darkness in it? Why are we faced with so many instances of failure, lack of faithfulness, and moral evil, even among some of the Church's leaders? We can acknowledge that there are many good people in the Church, and we can see that the Church has often exercised a beneficial influence on various aspects of life. But the same could be said for other human institutions. When we find that many of the Church's members behave no better than anyone else, and when we recognize that whatever good things Christianity has brought to the world, it has not been able to eradicate war and injustice or to bring about universal harmony and charity in the societies it inhabits, and when we notice that the Church cannot always even keep such ideals present and strong in its internal life, we can grow doubtful about its claims.

For serious Christians who love their faith and their Church, the sins and unfaithfulness of Christians can go beyond being a matter of concern and can attack their fundamental beliefs. Has something gone dreadfully wrong? Could it be that Christ is not really with the

Church in the way we have thought? Maybe the Christian answers to the problems of humanity are not really true? The result can be that discouragement, anger, and anxiety – none of them fruits of the Holy Spirit – often plague Church members.

This difficulty is understandable, but it is rooted in a false perception of what Jesus intended the Church to be, a perception influenced in no small way by utopian, neo-Gnostic strains of thought. What follows is a brief discussion of two key aspects of the Church that can help put things into proper perspective. The first is the truth that the Church is by necessity at the center of human history. The second is the truth that the battle to save humanity, the fight between Christ and the devil, between the Kingdom of God and the Kingdom of this World, has been mysteriously ordained by God to take place partly *inside* the Church. Understanding these two truths can help us take our proper strategic stance as we join Christ in the spiritual struggle of our time.

2. The Shock of the Incarnation

The best place to begin the discussion is with the astonishing claim at the heart of the Christian faith. Christians hold that the Being of beings, the Source of all that is, the One who created everything and who holds everything in existence, the One who made time itself and who is Master of all times and all destinies, once entered his creation, clothed himself in time, united himself to humanity, and lived among us to bring our wayward race back to life and goodness.

We can easily miss the shock of this claim when we think mainly in terms of a rational ordering of "comparative religions." The idea goes something like this: religion is a universal human phenomenon and shows up in many guises in different cultures. Individual expressions of the human religious instinct fall under the broad genus "reli-

gion" and share many similar qualities. Like the different languages of humanity, religions are local ways of expressing universal concepts and ideas, and however they might differ from one another, they all belong in the same category. Christianity is one among the rest. One can place important religious figures within a cadre of spiritual founders – Moses, Confucius, Mohammed, Buddha, Lao Tzu, and others we may think appropriate – and put Jesus into the mix. This way of proceeding has its advantages; there are after all many similarities among the world's religions. But it also hides a glaring fact: that the claims Jesus made about himself are so radically and momentously different from any other religious figure that they put him in a category entirely by himself.

The many founders and leaders of the world's great religions have presented themselves as humans addressing other humans. They have spoken on behalf of the divine as prophets or have pioneered a way of wisdom as sages. While Jesus took on the identity of both prophet and sage, he came among us as something immensely more. He made the astonishing and even outrageous claim that though he was a man, he was also God himself, the Creator of the universe and the origin of all existence, who had come to live among his creatures.

If this claim, that *"before Abraham was, I am"* (Jn 8:58), is true, it means that Christ is by necessity the absolute center of human history. To say this is not to indulge in a triumphalist Christian jingoism, insisting that Jesus is the top religious figure because he happens to be ours. It is not to suggest that Christians as individuals are better than other people. It is not to say that Jesus is the world's only figure of historical interest or significance. It is merely to draw the obvious conclusion from the astounding fact of the Incarnation. If it is true, as Christians hold, that the almighty and infinite God really did, once in history, visit the earth in bodily form, that he took on human

flesh, walked among us, and performed an act of cosmic significance that touches every human life, then that occurrence is by many orders of magnitude the most important thing that has happened since the creation of the world. It is *the* event that interprets everything else. As C. S. Lewis once observed with the claim of the Incarnation in mind, "One must keep on pointing out that Christianity is a statement which, if false, is of *no* importance, and if true, is of *infinite* importance. The one thing it cannot be is *moderately* important."[18]

3. The Church, Christ Incarnate Through Time

When we think of the Incarnation, we naturally and rightly think of those astonishing thirty-three years during which God lived among us as a man. But we can forget that the Incarnation of God's Word in Christ did not end with the Ascension. Christ continues to be mysteriously but genuinely present and incarnate in the world.

At the Last Supper, the disciples grew sad when Jesus told them he was leaving them, and he countered their disappointment with a promise: *"I will not leave you desolate; I will come to you"* (Jn 14:18). He then told them, surprisingly, that it was better for them that he go, that the Holy Spirit would be an improvement on his physical presence. They knew him then only outwardly as one person knows another, constrained by the limits of time, space, and the imperfections of mutual human understanding. But by the gift of the Holy Spirit, Jesus would dwell within their very minds and hearts. Their union with him would be less visible but more profound and more constant, richer and more real.

The Church calls itself the mystical body of Christ. The use of the word "mystical" indicates that the Church is not Christ's

---

[18] *God in the Dock*, "Christian Apologetics"

literal body with physical hands, feet, and head. But this is not just a fancy way of saying that Christians should be a close-knit group. The Church really is Christ's body; he is mysteriously present now in the Church, communally and in its individual members. Saint Paul spoke of Christ's individual presence when he said, *"I have been crucified with Christ; it is no longer I who live, but Christ who lives in me; and the life I now live in the flesh I live by faith in the Son of God, who loved me and gave himself for me"* (Gal 2:20). He pointed to Christ's communal presence when he said, *"He [Christ] is the head of the body, the Church"* (Col 1:18), and when he referred to the Church as *"the pillar and bulwark of the truth"* (1 Tim 3:15). When the Creeds call the Catholic Church "holy" as an article of faith, they are not describing the virtue of its human members, many of whom are far from holy. They are referring to the presence of the Holy Spirit as the principle of the Church's life and of Christ himself as the head of his body, the Church.

To bring this important truth into relief, it can help to note some of the ways the Church is often described or understood, but that fall short of its essence.

- The Church is not a society of like-minded individuals who have voluntarily gathered together for a common project.
- The Church is not a man-made, bureaucratic structure to help things along organizationally, a largely political body that goes forward by the same dynamics as other political and organizational groupings.
- The Church is not a humanitarian institution founded for the care of the poor, the sick, and others in need.
- The Church is not a utopian society with a blueprint for ordering human life according to perfect justice and peace (in the present age).

- The Church is not a democratic body that under[illegible] and determines its beliefs in keeping with the ide[illegible] majority of its members, or for that matter with the ideas of any minority of its members.
- The Church is not one religious grouping among others of a similar kind, a repository of spiritual experience and wisdom about meaning, morality, and how to cope with life, whose insights are to be sorted through and applied or rejected according to each individual's best lights.
- The Church is not a society of so many millions of people who happen to be alive at the moment, a body whose numbers fluctuate with the generations and whose fortunes change with the times, like nations and ethnic or racial groupings.
- The Church is not an archaic organization with an outmoded form of belief and practice that may once have served its time but is no longer suited to the needs and desires of modern people.
- The Church is not an unfortunate mistake, a human corruption of what should have been a purely spiritual and immaterial set of religious ideals and sentiments.

Some of these descriptions are simply false, and others touch on a true but limited aspect of the Church's nature. But none of them get to its heart, and all are seriously reductionist. They make the Church much smaller and more superficial than it truly is.

How then could the Church be described as it really exists? If our view should be opened upon what the angels see, what might we perceive?

- The Church is the New Humanity, the redeemed human race now sharing the life of God himself.
- The Church is a heavenly body pulsating with divine brightness and life, the majority of whose members are no longer

earthly mortals but part of a vast company who are now in God's presence or making their way to him through a process of purification.

- The Church is filled with the beauty and light of God and centered on the figure of Christ, who is head and bridegroom, ever leading and begetting new life within the Church. The fortunes of the Church are beyond the reach of anything on earth and are squarely in the hands of God.
- The vast majority of the Church's members need no faith because they are already home, sharing in delighted communion with God. They are not subject to death, and they experience no sin, no injustice, no scandal, and no imperfection. They have reached the destiny for which they were created.
- Angels are fellow members of the eternal Church: powerful beings reflecting and praising the goodness and light of God and incessantly carrying on a spiritual battle with forces of darkness, mighty spirits both in worship and in their help for humans.
- Mary, the queen of heaven and mother of the Church, is a figure of beauty and authority in the Church's life, eager to bring aid with tender pity to those of her children still languishing under the ancient curse. Under Christ's leadership, the twelve apostles continue to exercise their governing role in the Church, taking thought especially for their brothers and sisters who are still fighting for their place in the kingdom.
- Within the Church in heaven the great ones from every age are united together in friendship and joy, eager as each generation brings another rich harvest to the growing body of perfected humanity until the times are fulfilled and all are gathered in. And so the eternal Church is constantly growing, as its human members slip through the veil from this life to the next.

- The portion of the Church now existing in our space-time world and that consists of mortal humans – what has sometimes been called the Church Militant – is a colony of the heavenly Church on earth, an outpost of the great company, and through a thin veil is in constant communication, friendship, and communion with the angels and with the Church's perfected human members.
- This militant wing of the Church is a kind of resistance movement behind the lines of our ancient enemy, made up of souls who are being prepared for their true home and who are battling to live according to heavenly harmonies while witnessing to the truth of Christ for the sake of others. Through the Holy Spirit, Christ inhabits this portion of the Church and makes himself present to this world.
- The straggling human members of the Church on earth, we who are still broken, diseased, and in the process of healing, are the least numerous, least impressive, least potent, and least permanent part of the Church, inhabiting the outskirts of its life. We are still in a place of shadows, of ever-encroaching darkness and glimmering light. But we live in joy and hope because Christ himself is alive among us as physician, teacher, and king. He is leading us along our path to eternity, and we are already beginning to participate in the deathless life of our true home.

Blind to this high vision, the reductionist and worldly conception of the Church sometimes gives rise to this question: "The way things are going, will the Church be able to survive?" But when the reality of the Church's nature is perceived, rightly and truly, it becomes clear that there is no question of the Church "surviving." The Church is gloriously alive and beyond the reach of death. It is the fallen world that will not survive. It also becomes clear that the Church is at the center of this world's drama. Just as the whole of human history was

turning on the person of Jesus even when he was unknown and living in a small town in Galilee, so the whole of human history turns on the person of Jesus as he is present and working in and through the body he has chosen for himself, his Church.

4. The Divine and Human Church

As Christians know, Jesus was both divine and human. His human nature was available to all comers; those around him could see him, talk with him, and hear him speak. But his divine nature was hidden and not easy to perceive. *The Jews then murmured at him, because he said, "I am the bread which came down from heaven." They said, "Is this not Jesus, the son of Joseph, whose father and mother we know? How does he now say, 'I have come down from heaven'?"* (Jn 6:41-2). Jesus performed miracles as signs of his divinity, and those whose hearts were seeking God acknowledged him as Lord and Savior. But many, even most, of those who saw and heard him did not respond to him that way. Some viewed Jesus's miracles as interesting phenomena, a kind of impressive magic. Others wanted to kill him precisely because he performed miracles. *He casts out demons by the prince of demons* (Mt 9:34). Only with eyes enlightened by faith could Jesus be seen truly, as the divine Son of God.

The same phenomenon of sight and blindness that occurred when the Son of God was among us as a man also happens when we encounter the Son of God in the Church. Because the Church is Christ's body, it is both divine and human. The heart of the Church and its most important aspect (by far) is its divine nature: the presence of the Holy Spirit within it, the channel of saving graces flowing through the sacraments, the living fire of the Scriptures, the truths about God and humanity that are treasured and taught, and the enthralling personality of Christ at the core of its life that gives

form and purpose to everything it does. Yet that divine personality is made visible in the human aspect of the Church: each one of us and all the millions of Christians around the world, along with bishops and priests, religious orders, thousands of church buildings, and the many organizational, legal, and philanthropic structures that go into its life. Christ came to found a kingdom, and the Church on earth has many characteristics of a human kingdom – a polity and a social architecture that can be seen, touched, and interacted with, the outward clothing of its invisible, inward life. This is what is meant by calling the Church the sacrament of Christ.

Just as Jesus provided signs of his divinity when he was a man, so he continues to provide signs of his divinity within his mystical body, the Church. Among the greatest of these signs are the lives of the saints, those astonishing figures who are not merely noble humans, but men and women who have been transformed by divine life in humanly impossible ways. Other miraculous signs also continue to occur, such as healings, exorcisms, and fulfilled prophecies. Believers continually encounter Jesus in the Church's sacraments and in prayer and are given regular interior signs of his presence and protection. There are indications of divinity in the longevity of the Church, in its ability to continually recover and renew itself, in the consistency and fidelity of its teaching through the centuries, and in the ways it has touched individuals, peoples, and cultures across the globe.

Yet there is a special challenge in seeing the divine in the Church, a sharper difficulty perhaps than that of a first-century Jew seeing the divine in Jesus. Although Jesus shared our condition of humanity and all the consequences of our fall, he himself never sinned. In the Church, Christ has taken another step in his solidarity with fallen humanity by making his presence known through obviously sinful humans. When we encounter the human and sinful side of

the Church – the scandalously bad behavior of some, the mediocre spiritual life of many more, the often unimpressive and small-minded ways some in the Church go about their business, the faults and limitations of even its best members – it can be difficult for us to perceive the presence of Christ.

As with Jesus the man, so with Jesus in the Church: only faith can open our eyes to the presence of the divine mysteriously united to the human. Faith looks for the signs, hears the voice of God in the Scriptures, hungers for the bread of life in the Eucharist, and knows that Christ himself is present. Illuminated by the vision of faith, we see that the fate of the Church is not decided by appearance, by public relations, by political or social machinations and manipulations. It is not upheld by money, by influential connections, or by human laws. Any of these factors may play a secondary role in a given strategy that Christ is using, but the strength of the Church is found in its heavenly divine life. It is rooted in the eternal regions where it cannot be touched; it is animated by the life of God himself, inhabiting it as his body; and its militant wing is strong when its members are becoming holy, usually in hidden ways that no one can see. Without the vision of faith, all that can be seen is a gathering of humans and their various organizations and activities, humans who are often unimpressive and who are sometimes downright evil – humans like us.

5. Faith: Healing the Mind's Eye

We can sometimes think of faith as a particular feeling connected to those memorable times when we experience the powerful presence of God. Or we can think of it as a religious opinion that depends on the subjective experience of each individual who develops a "personal faith." Or we may think that to have faith is to hold blindly to a hope

or belief that we have no real grounds for: a leap into the dark. But these notions of faith are inadequate.

Saint Thomas Aquinas called faith "a habit of the mind, whereby eternal life is begun in us, allowing the intellect to assent to what is not seen."[19] Saint Catherine of Siena, a great mystic, received from the Lord a description of faith in similar terms: "The intellect, which is the eye of the soul, is illuminated by the knowledge of my truth. This eye of the soul has faith for its pupil and center, and the light of faith enables the soul to discern, to know, and to follow my truth – the Word incarnate. Without this pupil of faith the soul would not see, but would be like a person who has the form of an eye but who has covered the pupil of his eye with a cloth."[20] These descriptions of Thomas and Catherine echo a line from a passage in Saint Paul: *We look not to the things that are seen but to the things that are unseen; for the things that are seen are transient, but the things that are unseen are eternal* (2 Cor 4:18). Paul speaks of faith as a kind of vision, a way of seeing and understanding. The book of Hebrews calls faith *the conviction of things not seen* (Heb 1:1).

The gift of faith is the healing of our minds, giving us the ability to grasp what is real and true in its entirety. With our senses we can get a certain way into what is real, but the most important things – God, Christ in the Church, angels, the human soul – are invisible to us. The person who only knows what can be seen by the senses has been caught by a very narrow and illusory view of reality. The person who has been given the gift of faith acknowledges the visible world but sees much further. Faith takes that cloth spoken of by Saint Catherine away from our eyes; it broadens our minds and opens us out upon a vast and momentous universe.

---

19 *Summa Theologiæ* IIa-IIæ, q.4

20 *The Dialogue*, "The Treatise of Discretion"

As was true when Jesus walked the earth, God is still active and engaged in our world, pursuing his rescue mission with all the powers of heaven. As was true then, the most important events, the most powerful acts, the most significant developments going on around us and within us cannot be seen by human eyes, and are hidden especially from those blinded by unbelief. As was true then, so now: Jesus can be seen truly only with enlightened eyes, with eyes healed of their cataracts and astigmatisms, with eyes that have had the logs taken out of them, with eyes of faith.

6. In the Likeness of Sinful Flesh

The restored vision of truth brought about through the gift of faith reveals to us some very surprising aspects of God's way with us. Consider the heart of the Gospel message. We members of the human race, created by God for happiness, had become estranged from him by our rebellion against his plan and had brought spiritual death upon ourselves. We were now suffering from a self-inflicted wound that inevitably moved us toward evil, and our denial of God had delivered us into a grim slavery to dark powers too strong for us. In his mercy, our good God did not allow this situation to stand. The Scriptures never tire of speaking of the *kerygma*, the proclamation of God's saving work. Here is one expression among many found in Saint Paul:

> *God, who is rich in mercy, out of the great love with which he loved us, even when we were dead through our trespasses, made us alive together with Christ (by grace you have been saved), and raised us up with him, and made us sit with him in the heavenly places in Christ Jesus, that in the coming ages he might show the immeasurable riches of his grace in kindness toward us in Christ Jesus.* (Eph 2:4-7)

We know these articles of our faith, but our familiarity with them can lead us to forget just how unlikely, from a merely human point of view, was God's plan for the saving of our race. If we had been asked beforehand to guess at how an all-powerful and all-wise Lord of heaven would attack an earth dominated by evil spirits to bring freedom to an enslaved populace, we could imagine any number of possible scenarios. We might think of a frontal assault, a kind of D-Day invasion with flags flying and the enemy smashed and retreating. We might imagine a special-ops scenario by which a crack team of highly trained angelic operatives slipped under enemy radar and pulled off a daring rescue. But whatever plan we might have concocted, we could never have imagined what God actually did.

In his classic work *On the Incarnation*, Saint Athanasius wrote that God faced a kind of dilemma in his intention to save the human race. His problem was not a lack of strength to destroy the forces of evil. But there were two considerations that kept him from the simple use of coercive force. First, the only possible salvation for humans was to find a way to undo our original rebellion and reunite us in friendship and freedom to the source of love and goodness. Coercion might compel obedience, but that would leave humans in the stance of the demons, hating the One they were forced to obey and facing a stern sentence of justice for their evil actions. Only a willing turn from our rebellion could effect a cure. And second, there was a claim of justice that needed to be addressed. The human race was guilty of rebellion against Goodness himself, and justice needed somehow to be fulfilled. God's solution to this two-fold dilemma was to take the whole of humanity's destiny upon himself, such that what they needed to accomplish but could not – regaining their innocence and overthrowing their oppressor – he would do on their behalf as one of them.

To bring his plan to its successful conclusion, God chose a path that was not only unlikely, but that has been a scandal and a source of profound difficulty to skeptical humans ever since. It was a path that his own close disciples had a hard time understanding, because it seemed to turn everything they were expecting on its head. Saint Paul put it this way: *"For our sake God made him to be sin who knew no sin, so that in him we might become the righteousness of God"* (2 Cor 5:21). "God made him to be sin": Christ did not come among us in the form of a god-like superman, an obviously perfect person ministering to the imperfect, a supremely healthy specimen dispensing medicines to sick people, a figure of immense strength helping the weaklings around him. In truth he was all of that, and more, in his divine nature. But in becoming incarnate he clothed himself not only in our humanity, but in all the outward corruptions of our fallen humanity. *He had no form or comeliness that we should look at him, and no beauty that we should desire him* (Isa 53:2). *God has done what the law, weakened by the flesh, could not do, sending his own Son in the likeness of sinful flesh and for sin* (Rom 8:3).

Jesus contracted all the diseases of our race – not the moral guilt itself, but all the symptoms of our guilt. He was tempted by them, suffered from them, was sickened and afflicted by them, and was killed by them. He then destroyed them from within by rising from the dead, because his life was divine and could not ultimately be vanquished. He interiorized our evil in his own person and dissolved that evil even as he was seemingly crushed by it. In this very way, he generated an immunity in his blood, he developed the antibodies against our moral diseases, and he shared that medicine with his followers so that they too could triumph over their spiritual sickness and escape death. He then directed them to bring his healing remedy to an ailing race. This is the meaning of the Crucifixion: that

death has become the road to life; that from seeming defeat comes resounding victory.

7. Catching All the Diseases of the World

What Jesus began during his public ministry he has continued to do in his body, the Church. In every age, Christ in the Church addresses the diseases of the world by the process of crucifixion, by taking them upon himself and healing them from within his own body. He does this by speaking the truth in the midst of the world's deceptions, by enduring the hostility of those who love the darkness rather than the light (Jn 3:19), and by bringing light and salvation to the world through his suffering. This is what gives such significance to the Christian martyr: it is Christ again giving his life for the sake of the world. All Christians, as members of Christ, share in this mission to the degree that they witness to truth while struggling against evil and suffering for it, even cheerfully. This is a primary aspect of the first theater of warfare mentioned earlier. The *first front* of the "three-front Christian battle" is the struggle between the Church and the external forces of darkness. It is evangelization, the ever-necessary campaign to bring faith to an unbelieving world.

Yet there is a second theater of warfare, a *second front*, and it is perhaps more intensive and of greater strategic importance. It is the fight for truth on behalf of humanity that takes place *inside* the Church. The Church is at the heart of humanity, and it is within the Church that a decisive battle for humanity is taking place in every age. God surely loves all humans with an equal ardor and desires that all his creatures learn to know and love him. Yet his chosen way of saving humanity has been to select one people from among the rest who then become both his instrument of light to the world and,

mysteriously, the battleground where much of the fight for the souls of humans is waged. That battleground is now the Church.

Here it is possible to begin to see more clearly the ingenuity at work in God's plan. Just as Christ in his body of flesh contracted all the diseases of fallen humanity and generated the immunity in his blood, so also the Church – Christ's mystical body on earth – contracts the diseases of each age. The Church (through some of its members) is prone to catch the special diseases afflicting the human race in each generation, the current variant of the virus of error or the strain of moral corruption, the particular scandal of fallen humanity in a given time. The Church then suffers and grows sick, and once again a feverish battle takes place within the body of Christ. Afflicted and tempted in its members, the struggle and heartbreak are great. But, by the indwelling of the Holy Spirit, the Church possesses the spark of divine life. This ensures that the Church is never ultimately vanquished but instead overcomes each virus of error or sin, generating a costly immunity and priceless antibodies which it is then able to offer as medicine from its bloodstream to the world, so as to draw more and more of the rest of humanity into the experience of divine life: healed, healthy, free.

This recurring drama, tragic then triumphant, is a key element of the Church's mission. The Church has been chosen to fight this internal battle on behalf of humanity. We children of modernity, swimming in a sea of Progressive religion, will want to pay special attention to this quality of God's action. We live in an age of utopian belief that is constantly devising schemes for the perfection of the world. We can mistakenly come to think that Christianity is meant to be one more utopian program among them, a society of good and loving people who do not get seriously tainted by the world's sinfulness. Under that misconception, we can expect and insist that the

Church as a whole fly above all the world's imperfections, distant from its darknesses and free of its diseases. When we find that the ills afflicting the unbelieving world have wormed their way into some part of the Church, we can grow perplexed and discouraged, deeply angry and hopeless. We can repeat the utopian critique that "Christianity has been tried, and it didn't work."

Yet Christianity always works, according to the standard that God has established for it. How often has it happened during the two-thousand-year history of the Church that a priest at Mass, after praying the Eucharistic Prayer, has had to say to the congregation: "Sorry folks, it didn't work this time. Jesus didn't show up, and you'll just have to go home without your life-giving medicine. Come back next week and we'll try again"? When has the water of Baptism ever failed to do its work of imparting divine life to a dying soul? When has the Sacrament of Reconciliation ever failed to bring forgiveness and healing to a contrite penitent? When have the Scriptures ever failed in presenting the truth of God to a faith-filled member of his people or to an earnest seeker after truth? Christ in the Church never fails. The medicine of God has a one hundred percent success rate. It is the human element in the Church that often fails. We are the ones who will not take our medicine, who do not follow the divine physician's protocols, who stubbornly resist the action of God's grace. Yet this mingling of God's perfection and our imperfection, of God's utter goodness and our sinfulness, is our heavenly Father's chosen means of bringing the human race back to life. The inevitable struggle between light and darkness inside the Church is the drama of Christ's continuing work of salvation, as in every age and in each person he takes on the world's evil – our evil – and *becomes sin for our sake.* He then overcomes that evil in his own person, his body, the Church.

There is a mystery in this providential action. On the one hand, God makes clear that the Church is meant to be ruled by the harmonies of heaven, to be a light to the nations, a visible sign of his presence and his rule. The Scriptures from beginning to end never tire of urging believers to lead a life worthy of the calling they have received, to no longer live like those who do not know God, to let their light shine before men. This call is summed up in the constantly repeated injunction: *"You must be holy as I am holy"* (e.g., Lev 11:44-45, 19:2, 20:26; Dt 23:14; Mt 5:48; 1 Pet 1:16; et al.). And surely this call has been fulfilled in its measure in the millennia of the Church's life. God's people have been a light to the nations, and multitudes have found their way back to God under the protection of the Church's teaching and dispensing of grace.

Yet there is another seemingly contrary reality that has also been with the Church from its beginnings. Because the Church is set up as a heavenly society in the midst of a fallen world, its members necessarily face the temptation of conforming themselves to patterns of fallenness rather than obeying God's heavenly ways. In his permissive providence, God has allowed a certain measure of darkness to afflict portions of his own people and has used it to sharpen the faith and the fighting spirit of his true servants. In words attributed to Saint Teresa of Avila, "God writes straight with crooked lines." He takes what is in itself unmistakably evil, and he mysteriously brings good from it. The unlooked-for way by which Christ turned the dark betrayal of Judas into a part of his plan to bring light to the world has echoed in every age of the Church's life. What follows are a few instances, snapshots from salvation history, that give us glimpses of this mysterious action of God.

Snapshot 1: Israel, God's Chosen People

Before God had begun his work of salvation, the human race was enmeshed in a dire malady that covered the entire earth: the sin of idolatry, the worship of false gods rather than the One True God. If a right relation to God was to be restored to humanity, this vast and universal practice of idol worship had to be confronted and brought down. The obvious way to proceed might be to deal with the earth's idolatrous practices in one bold sweep across the globe, or to initiate a crusade for restoring true worship in the most populous and culturally developed centers of human civilization. Instead, God took the surprising road of calling one man, Abraham, and gathering together one small and unimpressive people, the Israelites. He then expended immense energy on them, drawing them into relationship with himself, establishing a covenant with them, and teaching them under his loving hammer blows to abandon their idolatrous practices and learn true worship.

The lesson was not easy for the Israelites to learn, and it took them many centuries to fully embrace it. While God regularly defeated Israel's external enemies, he was yet more intent on purifying his own people for the sake of their mission. The prophets were concerned less about the sinfulness of Gentiles than about the unfaithfulness and idol worship among God's own people. The Old Testament is mainly the story of God's battle against idolatry *inside* his chosen people, the Old Testament Church. That battle eventually led the Israelites to exile and near destruction, but the fruit of that bitter medicine was freedom from the sin of false worship; God's people had learned their lesson. When Jesus, the promised Messiah, arrived among the Jews,

the plague of idolatry was not among the sins he needed to confront. And the time was soon approaching when the worship of the one true God would be brought to the wider world under the banner of Christ. The dangers of idolatry were not thereby entirely removed, and false worship has continued to make its way under more subtle guises; but the explicit worship of evil spirits had been decisively dealt with in Israel.

Snapshot 2: "My mission is to the lost sheep of the house of Israel" (Mt 15:24).

It is a noteworthy fact that Jesus – God among us – spent virtually all of his time on earth with the Church, the house of Israel. He occasionally interacted with the unbelieving world as if to show that his love and mission were for all humanity, but his mode of reaching them was through his own people. Jesus did not attack the sins of Romans and Persians or oppose the corruptions of the Chinese or Indian civilizations. He did not go on a world-wide preaching tour, visiting important cities and wandering afar among nomads and forest dwellers. His ultimate plan was to gain all of them, but he did so by dealing first and primarily with the Jews. His fiercest battles were against the corruptions of Church people: Pharisees and Scribes, Kings and High Priests.

Here again we find God's way of dealing with us unlikely and hard to understand from a merely human point of view. When we think about changing the world – and if ever there was someone who planned to radically change the world, it was Jesus – our minds naturally go to centers of power and influence, to large movements involving vast numbers, and to maximum use of

communication. Yet the one whose coming changed all of human history was entirely unknown to the great world of his time.

Snapshot 3: The Gospel drama

In the cosmic drama at the center of human history – the Incarnation, death, and rising of the God-man, a drama that would affect the fate of every person who ever lived – God assigned most of the important parts to members of the Church, the Jewish people, both as heroes and as villains. Among the heroes: Jesus, obviously, was a Jew, as were Mary and the apostles, along with Mary Magdalene, Zacchaeus, Joseph of Arimathea, and Nicodemus. And the villains: Judas the betrayer was Jewish, along with the Pharisees, Caiaphas, Herod, and the crowd that shouted, "Crucify him!" The presence of Gentile characters like Pilate had an important significance, but at the time they hardly knew what was going on, and Jesus did not pay them much attention. His concern, wide as the human race, was focused first on the battle within the Church, among those he had chosen for his purpose.

What was true in the Gospel drama is true in the continuing battle for humanity. Christians have often been given the important parts in the drama of the human race: the best and the worst, the greatest heroes and the greatest villains, have been members of the Church.

Snapshot 4: The teaching of Jesus

Not only by his acts and the chosen circumstances of his life, but also by his explicit teaching, Jesus made clear that the Church

was to be a prime location of spiritual warfare, a continuation of the battle enjoined under the Old Covenant and brought to a climax in his own divine-human person. Just as Jesus was *made to be sin* for the sake of destroying sin, so the Church would have both weeds and wheat within it (Mt 13:24-30); there would be living and dead branches attached to the Vine (Jn 15:1-6); the sheep and the goats would both claim to be Christians and call out "Lord, Lord," but would have very different fates (Mt 25:31-46); and the kingdom would gather up all kinds of fish in its net, some to be kept and some to be thrown away (Mt 13:47-50). Jesus could hardly have been clearer about the human and sinful side of the Church. He taught his followers that the society he was establishing would exhibit both great holiness: *"Greater works than these will you do"* (Jn 14:12), and also great evil: *"Woe to the world for temptations to sin! For it is necessary that temptations come, but woe to the man by whom the temptation comes!"* (Mt 18:7). Jesus knowingly chose Judas as one of his picked men, as if to make clear that there would always be Judases, betrayers of Christ, at the highest levels inside the Church. He expected that the best and the worst of humanity were to be found within the Church. He said as much when he told the inhabitants of the sleepy fishing villages of Capernaum, Chorazin, and Bethsaida, members of his own people who were rejecting him, that they would fare worse on the day of judgment than the peoples of Sodom and Assyria, who were blatantly sinful pagans (Mt 11:24).

Snapshot 5: The battles of the early Church

The early disciples continued the fight Jesus had begun, often battling fiercely *inside* the nascent Church. Every book of the

New Testament addresses conflicts among the Christian people. Paul, Peter, James, John, and Jude were far more focused on struggles among Christians than on the evils of the wider world. When unbelievers were mentioned by them, it was either as those who needed to be converted: *Conduct yourselves wisely toward outsiders, making the most of the time. Let your speech always be gracious, seasoned with salt, so that you may know how you ought to answer everyone* (Col 4:5), or as those who were living obviously ungraced lives: *No longer live as the Gentiles do, in the futility of their minds; they are darkened in their understanding, alienated from the life of God* (Eph 4:17). It was not that the apostles were unaware of the need to battle the world's darkness. But they recognized that a key strategic battleground against that darkness would be inside the Church. From Ananias and Sapphira, to Simon Magus, to false apostles and teachers, the greatest concern and harshest words of the inspired authors, as of Christ their Master, were reserved for those corrupting the Church from within. Paul writes to Timothy: *"The Spirit expressly says that in later times some will depart from the faith by giving heed to deceitful spirits and doctrines of demons"* (1 Tim 4:1). And John writes in his first letter, *"Children, it is the last hour; and as you have heard that antichrist is coming, so now many antichrists have come; therefore we know that it is the last hour. They went out from us, but they were not of us; for if they had been of us, they would have continued with us; but they went out, that it might be plain that they all are not of us"* (1 Jn 2:18-19). These passages, from among many that could be cited, speak of the battle within the Church as a necessary aspect of spiritual warfare.

Snapshot 6: The history of the Church through the centuries

The same pattern can be seen throughout the history of the Church's life. The warning of Jesus to his disciples about the danger of salt losing its savor has rung in the ears of believers down the ages. Attentive to this strategy of the Master, Christians have been more vigilant about disobedience and heresy within the Church than the sins and infidelity of the wider world. It happens in every age that the Church, in some portion of its members, contracts the diseases of the time, and what often begins as a battle against an external opponent becomes an internal fight. Consider a few of the internal diseases that the Church has had to battle and that Christ mysteriously used for clarifying and solidifying its mission:

- The "Judaizing" tendency afflicting the early Church that sought salvation in the works of the Mosaic Law and that produced the medicine of Paul's teaching on grace and the decisions made at the Council of Jerusalem;
- The early Gnostic currents that denied the goodness of creation and emptied the meaning of Christ's crucifixion and that were healed by the medicines wrought out by great theologians like Irenaeus and Origen;
- The Arian error of seeking a philosophically pleasing alternative to the mystery of the Trinity that spread through the entire Church and that provoked the heroism of "*Athanasius contra mundum*," the medicine of the theological work of the Church Fathers, and the formulation of church creeds;

- The glorification of warfare and personal honor among the Germanic warrior peoples that led to the medicine of the chivalric code, theories of limited and just war, and the character of the Christian knight;
- The creeping worldliness afflicting the monastic world in the early Middle Ages that was countered by the medicine of the Gregorian reforms and the Cluniac and Cistercian revivals;
- The corrupting affluence of growing medieval cities that brought forth the medicine of Francis, Dominic, and the mendicant orders;
- The materialistic philosophies entering the bloodstream of the medieval universities that provoked the medicine of Albert the Great, Thomas Aquinas, and Bonaventure;
- The rampant power politics and worldliness among popes and bishops at the time of the Renaissance that instigated the medicine of the Council of Trent and new religious orders like the Jesuits, the Theatines, and the Oratorians;
- The unbelieving rationalism and violent revolution in the eighteenth century that sparked the medicine of liturgical renewal, of priestly reform in figures like John Vianney and John Bosco, and of deeper clarity around the relations between faith and reason and between the Church and the world worked out at the Vatican Councils;
- The current confusion concerning marriage and human sexuality that is stimulating a deeper understanding of the truths of human anthropology, making more explicit what for many generations of Christians has been implicitly believed.

In each of these cases, as in many others that could be cited, there have been currents abroad that have needed the healing and converting touch of Christ. It has been the work of Christ to address the wounds of fallen humanity with his divine medicine through the medium of his body, the Church, doing battle with his perennial truths against the characteristic falsehoods and moral diseases of the time; sifting and sorting each person and every culture in turn; raising up great saints, who through brave witness and in the crucible of suffering become themselves the healing antibodies in the Church's bloodstream; maintaining and strengthening what was good and rejecting what was evil. It is a process that is never complete or perfect in this age of the world. The task of conversion is ongoing, and the holiest and wisest among us are constantly being taken off to their reward, leaving the process to begin anew with each individual soul. Still, significant conversion has been brought about, and treasures have been laid down for the future and disseminated as leaven – but only after serious conflict inside the Church.

It is important to stress that those who have taken a leading part in fighting the Church's internal battles have done so with a good will. Though he was grieved, Jesus was not surprised or confused by Peter's denial, by Judas's betrayal, or by the resistance of the Chosen People to his message. Neither Saint Paul nor Saint John were shocked or dismayed by the fight they were waging, nor were any of the mighty battlers for the Faith, people like Irenaeus, Athanasius, Augustine, Thomas Aquinas, Catherine of Siena, Joan of Arc, Robert Bellarmine, Teresa of Avila, Bossuet, or Newman. They took it as a matter of course. They did not think that the Church's internal battle was a waste of their time or a distraction from their real business. They had learned from Jesus that this fight was exactly their real business.

V

Fighting the Battle Inside the Church

"I know that after my departure fierce wolves will come in among you, not sparing the flock; and from among your own selves will arise men speaking perverse things, to draw away the disciples after them."

— Saint Paul the Apostle[21]

"The warfare which Christ began between his little flock and the world was in no little time transferred into the Church itself, and was carried on by members of that Church with one another."

— *Saint John Henry Newman*[22]

WHATEVER MIGHT BE HAPPENING in the Church, in the world, or in our own lives, we will want to remember that God is not worried, perplexed, or defeated. His ways are not our ways, and we cannot always tell exactly what he is up to or how he is at work; but faith, true sight, assures us that he is the ultimate Master of all events. The world belongs to God even if it is in a state of rebellion against him, and he takes the responsibilities of ownership seriously. The Church even more so belongs to Christ as he inhabits it by the

21 Acts 20:29-30

22 *Parochial & Plain Sermons.* Vol 3, #15: "Contest between Truth and Falsehood in the Church"

Holy Spirit. Christ is the Church's main actor, its grand strategist, its motive and attractive power, and the only reason it can exist at all. Our task, individually and communally, is to try to understand what God in Christ is doing and to cooperate with him as best we can.

If we understand the way God is waging his warfare against darkness, we will not be surprised to find the Church in the midst of an internal battle. We will not be perplexed to find that some of its members, including some among its leaders, have followed the path of Judas and betrayed Christ. This has happened in past ages, and so it will happen in our own time. Understanding this reality is not meant to produce a complacent or fatalistic attitude toward corruption or unbelief within the Church. The opposite is true. It is precisely within the Church that we are meant to fight a zealous and determined battle for truth and goodness.

How is that battle to be best engaged? That question brings us to the third theater of warfare, the *third front* of the Christian spiritual battle. It was noted that the first front is the external fight against the darkness of the world. Activities on that front include such things as evangelistic initiatives, the daily Christian witness even to the point of martyrdom, and the various ways the Church leavens the social and cultural worlds it inhabits and moves them toward truth and goodness. The second front is the internal battle against the darkness of a fallen world as it finds its way into the Church. In matters dealing with corruption of Church teaching and governance or with sinful behavior among clerical and lay Church leaders, the responsibility for engaging that battle will by necessity fall most heavily upon those who are in positions of authority and influence. Jesus dealt decisively with the Chief Priests, Scribes, and Pharisees, the leaders of the Church of his day. When they had gone astray, he rebuked them and called them to task, as was fitting for

the Chief Shepherd in dealing with his under-shepherds. But he did not urge most of his followers to take upon themselves the same task of rebuking Church leadership, as if it were a part of their divine commission. His first counsel to his disciples in dealing with bad leadership was that they should beware false teaching (Mt 16:12) and stay on the alert against false prophets (Mt 7:1). When it was a question of bad behavior among Church leaders, he taught them to honor their position but to be careful not to imitate their behavior: *"Practice and observe whatever they tell you, but not what they do; for they preach, but do not practice"* (Mt 23:3). His general direction was that the disciples should stay away from bad leaders and leave them to be dealt with by God. When the disciples told Jesus that his teaching was offending the Pharisees, he said to them: *"Every plant which my heavenly Father has not planted will be rooted up. Let them alone; they are blind guides. And if a blind man leads a blind man, both will fall into a pit"* (Mt 15:13-14). Some among the Church's members will be called by God to wage this battle explicitly on behalf of the whole Church. But for most of us the main spiritual battle is elsewhere, and we can become distracted from our real fight by getting engrossed in matters for which we have been given no responsibility and that we can do very little to change.[23]

The third front of the spiritual battle, and both the primary arena and the necessary condition for gaining victory in both the world and the Church, is the struggle demanded of each of us against the darkness in our own hearts and minds. God's kingdom is established on earth mainly by personal conversion and holiness: the saints are the true movers and shakers of history. The grip of the

---

[23] An apt and very helpful meditation on when and how rightly to bring correction to others can be found in Newman's sermon, "Rebuking Sin" (*Parochial & Plain Sermons.* Vol 2, #24).

devil on the world is weakened far more effectively by acts of self-denial, charity, humility, and faith than by social and political action, however important and even necessary those activities are. Our most pressing practical concern in waging the spiritual battle is to ask how we, each one of us, might be more deeply converted in thought and action to the truth of Christ and ever freer from the false gospels that surround us.

If it is true that the Church tends to catch the diseases of the world and that the most potent religious disease currently afflicting us is the family of neo-Gnostic faiths we have been calling Progressive religion, we will want to be especially alert to the ways that we have been infected, whether overtly or subtly, by ways of seeing, understanding, and acting that stem from the distorted lens of Progressive religion, and how we can adjust our ways of seeing and acting according to the life and teaching of Christ.

What follows is a short list of suggested areas to examine as we walk our road to the kingdom in our current cultural atmosphere, what might be called an examination of vision and understanding.

1. The Embrace of a Different Gospel

The most obvious expression of the disease of Progressive religion inside the Church is found in those who profess to be Christian but who have abandoned key doctrines of the faith and have embraced some form of the neo-Gnostic gospel of personal self-creation. Examples of this kind of unbelief are rife in the current Christian world. In such cases one is dealing not so much with Christians who are to some degree under the influence of non-Christian beliefs, but with people who subscribe to Progressive religion and are no longer Christian in any meaningful sense, while continuing to use Christian language and maintain membership and even positions of

responsibility in the Church. This is a crucial battle to engage, but we will not be spending much time on it here, partly because many in the Church are aware of the problem and are working to clarify the Church's witness to the truth, and also because, as just noted, most of us are not in a position to seriously address the problem and can easily be distracted by it from more pressing battles closer to home. Our concern here is rather to uncover ways that even serious and faithful Catholics can unwittingly take on erroneous modes of thinking and seeing that stem from Progressive faiths.

To understand the sources of obvious unbelief inside the Church, it can help to remember that Progressive religion also offers a kind of salvation to its followers. Christians, who believe the Good News brought by Jesus Christ, know that they have a glorious Savior who is the source of all goodness, and they have placed all their hope in his promises. They are not on the lookout for another and more effective savior or a better gospel. It is different with neo-Gnostic Progressive believers inside the Church. It is likely enough that they were never genuinely converted to Christianity in the first place. They were perhaps hereditary Christians who were baptized as infants and grew up in a vaguely Christian home, who learned the basics of human morality through Church teaching, and who have retained an attachment to the outward symbols of the faith. But it is probable that they had never encountered the risen Christ as their Lord and Savior. This lack of conversion to the Gospel would leave them vulnerable to the allure of a different gospel promising a different salvation. At some point along the way, it could easily happen that such a person might succumb to one of the Progressive gospels so atmospherically prevalent around us. It is thus not surprising to encounter this type of unbelief dressed up in Christian clothing. Yet it should be a cause of concern to us that so many of the Church's

present and former members fall into this category of pseudo-faith, and that it is not unusual for a person to grow up in the Church and never to be seriously confronted with Christ's call. It points to our need to be more converted ourselves, and to develop apostolic strategies in our homes, schools, and parishes, such that the Gospel can be heard and experienced in all of its dynamic potency.

But what about more subtle ways that believing Christians can be catechized by the religion of the world rather than by Christ, and as a result can develop a skewed vision of reality? In previous sections, we laid out aspects of Progressive religion in their strong and clear form. What follows is a brief look at some areas where a more subtle infection can occur, contributing to a dimming of Christian faith and a weakening of Christian hope, even among those who are doing their best to follow Christ.

2. The Temptation to Pride

There is nothing new in the temptation to pride; it is as old as Adam and Eve. Yet there is a particular expression of pride that characterizes our time.

The classic picture of the prideful person is the haughty and arrogant type who strides the earth with his nose in the air, paying little attention to the needs of others and thinking himself better than the rest of the world. Most modern people are not prideful in that sense. For complex reasons that have to do with the social and technological fluidity of modern life, most of us who inhabit the modern world lack a strong sense of identity, and far from thinking too highly of ourselves, we often struggle to think ourselves even as good as other people. As a result, we gravitate toward externally generated and often superficial sources of identity that bolster our lack of personal confidence. In our fragility, we are easily wounded

by negative opinions from others, and we become obsessed by the desire not to offend anyone. This situation would seem to point not to pride, but to an excess of humility. Yet at the same time, we swim in a cultural sea of Promethean defiance toward everything divine. Our world takes it as a given that it is up to each individual person to order his or her existence, choose a morality, and decide upon the meaning of life, all without recourse to a Creator. Catch-phrases like "You can be whatever you want to be," or, "Your life is your own and no one else's," despite being profoundly illusory, are so common as to be uncontroversial. We assume that the hard-won experience of our ancestors and the long wisdom of our intellectual and cultural traditions have little to teach us concerning how to live a morally good life. We view the universe as so much random chaotic matter to be manipulated and exploited in the interests of our plans and desires and have little sense for a cosmic order that needs to be honored if we are to find goodness and happiness. This places all of us in an historically anomalous situation. We moderns suffer from a kind of visionary schizophrenia. In our experience of ourselves we are among history's most fragile and unconfident humans, while in our approach to all things divine we are among the most prideful people the world has ever known. This odd combination points to a key challenge for Christians of our time: how to stir up magnanimity, courage, confidence, and high ideals on the one hand, and on the other how to regain a humble and therefore true stance toward God.

When theologian Romano Guardini posed the question: "What is the presupposition for all moral effort to be effective, to change what is amiss and to strengthen what is weak?" he gave this answer: "It is the acceptance of what is, the acceptance of reality, your own

and that of the people around you and of the time in which you live."[24] Guardini was speaking of a stance of humility toward reality. In embracing this attitude, we are imitating Jesus himself. Jesus entered our world with the goal of radically transforming it, but he began by accepting its conditions and limitations, including its sinfulness. He knew that the possibility of evil was within his Father's permissive will, a result of the freedom God had granted to humanity. He was not angry, frustrated, or defiant at the fact of a fallen world. He was not in a state of rebellion against reality, which would have meant prideful resistance to the Father and his goodness. Jesus's acceptance of reality was emphatically not a stance of complacency or of cooperation with evil. He planned to utterly change and renew the world. But he knew that the only effective way to accomplish that purpose was to work within the Father's created order and according to the Father's will.

3. Soft-Pedaling the Fall

We have observed that Progressive religion begins with and is founded on a denial of the Fall, or more precisely, a denial of our personal implication in the guilt of a fallen world. Serious Christians do not usually explicitly deny the doctrine of original sin, but under the pervading pressure of Progressive dogma, the reality of being fallen and the consequences that necessarily stem from that reality often cease to operate as living truths for us. We can unconsciously assume the Progressive dogma that people are fundamentally good – not just created in goodness and with a capacity for goodness, but good right now. We can imbibe the view that while everyone has faults and weak points, people on the whole are decent and well-

---

[24] *Learning the Virtues*

meaning, and it is just the few extreme cases who are really bad. But to think this way is to set aside the mind of Christ, who would not entrust himself to humans because *he knew what was in man* (Jn 2:25), and who did not hesitate to say to his beloved disciples, "*If you*, who are evil, *know how to give good things to your children...*" (Mt 7:11). It is to reverse Jesus's solemn admonition and assume that the road that leads to eternal life is wide and easy and many travel it, while the road that leads to destruction is narrow, difficult, and only possible for a few choice specimens. It is to ignore the terrible cost God had to pay in order to undo our sin. It is to forget that God does not love us because we are good, but in order to restore us to the goodness he originally intended for us.

It might seem an overly negative and dark picture of humanity to insist so forcefully on the evil consequences of the Fall. We might ask: after all, isn't it true that most people are basically decent, helpful, and oriented to goodness? Don't we have a regular experience of this in our normal social interactions? In response, it is good to remember certain factors that help to make the Scriptural picture more accessible. For one thing: we are living in a world that has been drenched in God's teaching and wisdom for thousands of years. Much of what we take for granted as normal human behavior – being kind to the needy and poor, avoiding cruelty, recognizing the basic rights of all people – was anything but normal before the coming of Christ. Even modern atheistic ideologies are living off the capital of Judeo-Christian beliefs for their moral ideas, though they do not usually know it. For another thing: the majority of people in our society have been baptized. Many are not living up to their baptismal call, but they are still benefitting from the restraint Baptism places on demonic activity. That restraint has allowed us moderns to think that we are inherently morally superior to previous ages. As the number of baptized people

has been diminishing in the West, cases of demonic possession have been skyrocketing; exorcists are busier now than they have been in centuries. And further: most people want to get along in life without too much conflict or difficulty, and if social circumstances are more or less favorable, the majority will be outwardly law-abiding and cooperative. Thus, the deepest orientations of the human heart, for both good and evil, are usually hidden from the public eye. The test comes when those comfortable social relations break down, as in a prison camp or a state of anarchy with no enforcement of law. Then the often-hidden state of the human heart comes to the light. Both great heroism and horrific cruelty and selfishness make themselves known at such times, and we hardly need to ask which is the more prevalent. All this, hidden from us, is plain to the sight of God.

When we fail to see the depth of individual human corruption, the Good News loses much of its potency and needs to be re-translated to keep our interest. As our awareness of sin fades and the idea of universal salvation becomes an unconscious assumption in our minds, the awe-inspiring figure of Christ – Lord of the Universe, the divine warrior who battled the prince of darkness, and who by an act of unfathomable love and suffering brought to his followers forgiveness of sin, freedom from demonic slavery, and the gift of eternal life – gets lost in favor of a different Jesus: the nice guy, the non-threatening personal life-enhancer who offers his followers wealth, wellness, self-realization, and a therapeutic program for coping with personal challenges. In such a scenario there is little at stake in following Christ and much less motivation to be grateful to God. Jesus once said, *"He who is forgiven little, loves little"* (Lk 7:47). If we do not know the immensity of our moral wound and the depth of what we have been forgiven, we will find genuine love and gratitude hard to come by, and the true Gospel meaning of freedom will be

subtly replaced by this-worldly notions of mere temporal betterment according to Progressive religious categories.

4. Forgetfulness of the Cosmic Order

Christians have been taught that God created a harmonious universe filled with meaning and dancing to a cosmic harmony. Dante ends his *Commedia* in the delighted contemplation of "the love that moves the sun and the other stars."[25] Meaning is written into our minds and consciences and into our physical makeup. Liturgy aligns us with that order of love and truth. Our way of handling food, sex, and the natural world are meant to reflect and express God's cosmic meaning. Our relations with one another are intended to replicate and participate in the inner life of the Trinity. Christians understand that the tragedy in which we have all been implicated has much to do with our race's unwillingness to embrace God's divine order, and that the only way to make the world a better place is to come back to a proper relation with God and creation, to regain our true voices so that we can once more enter the heavenly harmonies.

Under the constant barrage of neo-Gnostic dogma that denies or deplores the given order of things and attempts to refashion the structure of the world according to humanly devised theories, Christians can allow their vision of the cosmic order to get blurred. We can forget that our fulfillment is found in learning the steps of the divine dance, and we can subtly accept the notion that we will find happiness by constructing our own world of meaning. This can leave us baffled by Progressive appeals to self-creation and self-definition and thus unable to deal meaningfully and confidently with them, because our minds are not grasping that those appeals are based on

---

25 *Paradiso* 33.145

the assumption that there is no harmonious order to the world and no provident God who created each of us with purpose. This vulnerability can be seen especially in matters dealing with the divine order as expressed in human sexual identity and relationships.

An unconscious influence of Progressive religion can manifest itself in the vaguely irritated attitude that can creep into the minds of Christians who experience their faith as mainly a burdensome set of seemingly arbitrary "rules" that restrict human freedom. We can resent all these directives as unnecessary and as getting in the way of our happiness. A truer vision would perceive and acknowledge that God never gives us arbitrary or meaningless rules. In everything Christ teaches he is aligning us to truth and goodness. He is leading us out of disease into health, out of moral chaos into moral integrity, out of lies and deception into reality, out of dissonance and ugliness into harmony and beauty, out of the disorder of selfishness and rebellion into the cosmic dance of love, out of death into life. The joy of getting re-aligned to heaven's bright beauty explains something of the Psalmist's rapturous outburst toward God's commands: "*The law of the LORD is perfect, reviving the soul; the precepts of the LORD are right, rejoicing the heart… More to be desired are they than gold, even much fine gold; sweeter also than honey and drippings of the honeycomb!*" (Ps 19:7-8; 10). Christians who have a hard time saying that they love God's law may be laboring under a loss of the sense of cosmic harmonies.

5. The Myopia of Secularity

The Christian vision of life encompasses a horizon that goes far beyond the short and inevitably difficult few years that we call a person's lifetime. Seen truly, our time on earth is something like the life of a baby in the womb. It is of great importance, but it is not

an end in itself. It is a time of preparation for our real life and can only be understood in the context of where it is leading and what is coming after it. Modern Progressive faiths limit their vision of the world to what can be seen. They attempt the impossible feat of making sense of a human life within the brief compass of birth and physical death. The only heaven they can conceive of is one that is experienced here and now.

Christians seldom deny the fact of the immortal human soul or suggest that there is nothing beyond the grave; to do so would be to make the Christian faith nonsensical. Yet it is perilously easy for us, given a culture obsessively fixated on the seen and the temporal, to forget the primacy of the unseen and eternal and to act as though our hope was for this life alone. We have become experts in the art of visible distraction; we fill our eyes and ears with a constant stream of diverting content; we so speed up the pace of life that an atmosphere of peace and silence, so necessary for an awareness of the unseen world, is ever harder to come by. Under the constant pressure of a Niagara of sensual and informational distraction, we can be caught by the illusion that puts physical health ahead of spiritual health. We can get lost in the fog that counts economic prosperity as the main goal of life. We can be afflicted by the blindness that views human suffering and tragedy in this world as final and irreparable. We can subtly re-translate and reduce the Gospel into a this-worldly remedy for temporal poverty, sickness, and injustice. It is hardly surprising that in such an environment, believers have a hard time keeping their gaze on the deeper realities opened up by faith.

The symptoms of this kind of blurred vision show up in many ways and hardly need pointing out. As one example, it has been a noteworthy quality of Christianity that it frees its adherents from the fear of death; Christ came to *deliver all those who through fear of*

death were subject to lifelong bondage (Heb 2:15). Early apologists for the faith could point to this quality among Christian believers as a known fact. The ancient Roman world could not deny that Christian men, women, and even children faced martyrdom with remarkable courage and calm and could not be bribed or bullied into trading away eternity with God for the comparative trifle of a few years of mortal life, often even singing as they went to their deaths. None of this made any sense from the standpoint of this life alone; the treasure of those early Christians, along with their hearts, were where they belonged, in heaven. Could that claim about Christians still be made today? Does the world around us have to admit, perhaps grudgingly, that we are not intimidated or frightened by the prospect of death? That while we view bodily health as of some value, we hold that godliness is far more important, since it holds promise for the present life and also for the life to come (1 Tim 4:8)? That we count the most impressive prizes of this world as so much rubbish compared to the surpassing worth of knowing Jesus (Phil 3:8)?

6. The Utopian Drift

The last many centuries have seen the whole of our culture embrace a general utopian attitude toward life on earth, an understandable stance once the doctrine of the Fall is no longer in play. Utopia can sometimes refer to a state of things in which everything will be perfect in a dream world of fun and fulfillment. In that sense, most Progressive believers are not utopians. They acknowledge that absolute earthly perfection is an unattainable ideal. What makes Progressive religions utopian is their belief that there is no moral wound in each human heart that tends toward evil, and that therefore the possibilities for human betterment have no intrinsic limit. Though perfection may never be completely attained, there is nothing

keeping us from getting ever nearer to it. Psychology will sort out our inner world; sociology will show the way to peaceful relational harmony; political science will do away with war; economics will eradicate poverty; and scientific technology will make life on earth pleasurable and will extend our lifespans indefinitely. Nothing stands in the way of our advance toward an ever more perfect happiness except the reactionary elements of humanity that refuse to embrace the age of freedom and are stuck on the wrong side of history.

A necessary result of the Progressive utopian vision is the conviction that political action is the primary means by which the world will arrive at its desired goal. For Progressive believers, politics is not a secondary, if important, realm of human activity where compromise is often demanded for the sake of social concord. It is instead the central concern, the main arena of religious warfare, the key battleground for gaining control of the levers of power that will allow the implementation of proper knowledge for the saving of the planet.

Christians, who know that the world is made up of fallen creatures and is under the significant influence of the devil, and who are *waiting for new heavens and a new earth in which righteousness dwells* (2 Pet 3:13), do not therefore cease to work for the world's betterment here and now. Christians have always been concerned about the political and cultural order, since it touches on justice and human relations. They know that Christ's life and light can make a significant difference in how things go for individual people and for whole societies. They know that temporal happiness can be more widely disseminated and human suffering significantly curtailed by addressing the architecture of social life. They attempt where possible to see truth, justice, and peace furthered and evil kept at bay. What they do *not* do is set their hope on fixing the world by human means alone or on replacing the one we have with a better working model.

They know that they cannot get at the true root of the world's evil through political and cultural change and that the ultimate destiny of our visible world hangs on far higher invisible realities. They understand that we will neither be saved nor finally defeated by political and social developments.

Yet Christians are not untouched by the reigning utopian atmosphere; we often carry unconscious utopian assumptions that color our ability to gain the mind of Christ. Under the influence of the utopian drift, we can come to expect things to go basically well for us, and we can grow shocked and surprised when they do not. We can assume that the world should be getting ever better, not just technologically or materially, but morally. We can unconsciously come to believe that the moral problems of humanity are solvable by human effort. We can place our primary loyalty in a given political order and can invest the proximate realm of politics with ultimate significance. We can forget about the dark spiritual beings who exercise a decisive influence on world affairs. We can then be subject to discouragement when it seems that things may not be getting better and may even be getting worse. And when our vaguely utopian gaze shifts to the Church, we can come to expect that the Church will not be tainted by the world's ills, and we can grow demoralized by the sinfulness of many of its members.

All of this makes the practice of Christian hope difficult. The false and unattainable hope of Progressive religion is the hope of ultimate perfection in our temporal world. It is therefore no wonder that there is so much anxiety and despair around us. Christians should know better. Saint Peter writes: "*Gird up your minds, be sober, set your hope fully upon the grace that is coming to you at the revelation of Jesus Christ*" (1 Pet 1:13). Having renounced the proud utopian dream that bypasses human sinfulness and the devil's power, Christians will not

become discouraged or confused when they encounter great evil in the world or find that things do not seem to be getting better. They will continue, day by day, to work for justice, to help those in need, and to seek genuine peace, motivated by charity and for the sake of witness, keeping their hope where it belongs and leaving the results of their efforts in God's capable hands.

7. The Lure of the Silver Bullet

We noted earlier that Progressive religion is founded on the confidence that a rigorously applied social or psychological technique or program, united to increased technological mastery of the physical world, will solve our problems and save us. This mechanistic and simplistic approach to human life and human problems can seep into the consciousness of Christians, who then become vulnerable to constructing spiritual techniques of various kinds that will guarantee the desired Christian outcomes. We can fall prey to the idea that if we can just find the right program, if we can just figure out the effective formula, if we can only settle on the proper technique, we can deal with whatever challenges the Church is facing. We can forget that there is no sure-fire program to solve the human problem of evil – or rather, that the one "program" that will accomplish this has been revealed by Christ and involves Baptism, mystical incorporation into the Church, and the long, slow battle for holiness. We can look for superficial results that can be metrically quantified and neglect the real but mostly invisible internal battle that can only be won by a personal struggle against self and the demonic world. This is not to say that Christians should not try to find sound and effective means of proceeding or should not hold themselves to high standards of competence. But in rightly looking for the best ways to organize our social and cultural worlds and to order our life and mission in

the Church, we will want to remember that there is no system that cannot be corrupted, no set of protocols that cannot be perverted to the devil's use, and no simple remedy whose implementation will drive away human suffering, ensure social justice, convert the nations, or guarantee Christian holiness.

8. Seeing the World with Dualistic Eyes

We have seen that neo-Gnostic religions posit two radically distinct kinds of humans: the good people, or those who have embraced the correct Progressive dogma, and the evil people, or those who are standing athwart the progress of humanity.

Christians immersed in a Progressive religious environment can become infected by the same dark dualistic error. The command to love one's enemies can easily fall by the wayside, along with the understanding that *we are not contending against flesh and blood, but against the principalities, against the powers, against the world rulers of this present darkness, against the spiritual hosts of wickedness in the heavenly places* (Eph 6:12). This does not mean that Christians are naïve about human participation in evil. In the unfortunate state of our race, many sad souls have given themselves over to evil in profound ways and have made themselves enemies of Christ, and Christians regularly need to oppose them. Yet we have been given the difficult task of imitating our Master in regularly battling against humans while never allowing ourselves to be overcome by hatred for them. Saint Augustine once observed that the Scriptures often say that God would destroy his enemies. He then pointed out that God's preferred and most effective way of destroying his enemies was to turn them into his friends. Every Christian has made the transition from being an enemy of God to becoming his friend, and we should desire that the same blessed event happen even for our worst enemies, however unlikely it may seem in a given case.

The neo-Gnostic dualistic mindset can also insinuate itself into the way Christians battle for the faith inside the Church. Instead of viewing the sins of Christians and the failures of Christian leaders as God's judgment on an unfaithful people, as they are shown to be by the Scriptural prophets, the Christian who has been unduly touched by the Gnostic disease can separate the Church into "we good ones" and "those bad ones." We can become prey to conspiracy theories – a typical symptom of the Gnostic desire to gain control of the world by figuring everything out – and we can speak of the Church's being "infiltrated" by bad people. We can come to think that if we could just eradicate those Judases in the Church, we would finally become the pure and holy body we wish to be. We forget that Christ regularly warned us against such a view, and that if such a Church were ever genuinely to come into existence, the first thing it would do is throw sinners like us out of it. The proper response of Christians to the Church's sinfulness is shown to us by the prophet Daniel, whom the Scripture calls a righteous man, and who prayed in solidarity with God's unfaithful people. His prayer was: *"Forgive us Lord, for* we *have sinned"*; not: *"Annihilate them Lord, for* they *have sinned"* (Dan 9).

9. Using the Enemy's Weaponry to Fight the Lord's Battles

Saint Paul writes to the Corinthians: *"Though we live in the world we are not carrying on a worldly war, for the weapons of our warfare are not worldly but have divine power to destroy strongholds"* (2 Cor 10:3-4). Paul is making a practical strategic point. The whole of the Scripture makes clear that, though composed of the stuff of this world, the kingdom established by God is founded on sources of strength and proceeds by dynamics very different from the way things proceed

in the world. If Christians attempt to build God's kingdom as if it were a merely human thing, their attempts will be futile, and their ultimate failure will be certain. *"My kingship is not of this world,"* said Jesus to Pilate. *"If my kingship were of this world, my servants would fight that I might not be handed over to the Jews; but my kingship is not from the world"* (Jn 18:36).

In a world dominated by Progressive religious dogma, Christians need to be careful not to unconsciously embrace the weapons and tactics of the world in building the kingdom of God. One way this happens is to view the Church as primarily a political and sociological entity and to think that the prosperity of the Church will be assured by clever political maneuvering and well-crafted public relations. When people want to get something in the world to happen, they exercise various kinds of force, whether coercive or persuasive. It might be guns, or ad campaigns, or political action, or economic incentives, or stirring up people's passions, or impressing people with talent, cleverness, and displays of intelligence. We can think it natural that God's kingdom operates according to the same dynamics. We can assume that we need to use the same means – baptized of course and not in fundamentally unjust ways – to establish and maintain the faith and the Church. We can think it will be money, influence, talent, political power, and intelligence that will keep the Church alive and thriving. It is true that God can and does use these means for his own purposes. But he goes out of his way to make clear that these are not the ways his kingdom fundamentally grows. To gain a supernatural kingdom we need to use supernatural means.

Another way that Christians can be catechized by neo-Gnostic religion is by taking up the Progressive evangelistic mindset. Our fallen world is ruled by passion and almost always tries to influence people and enlist them in a pet cause by appealing to one of the

passions, whether the promise of physical pleasure, comfort, and wealth, or by disseminating anger and anxiety.

Christ did not spread his Gospel by inflaming the passions of his hearers. He did not lure them by promises of an easy life or dangle before their eyes this-worldly wealth and popularity; the prosperity gospel will find no resonance in the New Testament. *In the world you have tribulation; but be of good cheer, I have overcome the world* (Jn 16:33). At the same time, though, Jesus saw and understood evil better than anyone who has ever lived, and though he was treated with profound injustice, he was not an angry or an anxious man, and he was not interested in getting his hearers anxious or angry. His disciples were to be the bearers of a message of peace with God and hope of eternal life. As Saint James put it: *"Let every man be quick to hear, slow to speak, slow to anger, for the anger of man does not work the righteousness of God"* (Jas 1:1-20). To the degree that Jesus aroused fear in his hearers, it was the effect of a mind and conscience being touched by truth and recognizing its perilous state. The goal was repentance, a return to God, and then the exalted joy of new life. This is not to say that emotion and passion have no place in the Christian life, nor is it to suggest that there are not many aspects of a fallen world that tend to provoke anger. It is rather a question of what is leading and what is following. Our emotions are meant to follow the perception of truth and to support what truth and goodness demand. When Jesus saw people following him from excitement or anger, he would purposely get in the way of their passions. When multitudes were running after him entranced at the miracles he was doing, he stopped them in their tracks with a difficult teaching: *"If any one comes to me and does not hate his own father and mother and wife and children and brothers and sisters, yes, and even his own life, he cannot be my disciple"* (Lk 14:26). When James and John were angered by

the bad reception they were receiving from inhospitable Samaritans and wanted to call down fire from heaven on them, Jesus rebuked them (Lk 9:54).

Saint Paul explains the real motivating power behind the Christian stance toward the world: *The love of Christ controls us, because we are convinced that one has died for all; therefore all have died* (2 Cor 5:14). It was love that led the Father to send his Son to save us; it was love that motivated Jesus in all his dealings with our fallen race; it was love that led him to the Cross; and it is love that moves us to continue that saving rescue mission. Christians who settle into an angry posture are an anomaly, a counter-witness to the truths of Christ. Yet how easy it is for modern Christians to imitate the patterns of Progressive religion and come to be characterized largely by their anger. Instead of nurturing a fellowship of charity in Christ, we can find ourselves uniting in a fellowship of anger against human enemies, eager to keep up with the most recent examples of their unfaithfulness and quick to want to gather with others around common hatreds, and motivating our fellow Christians mainly by getting them anxious and enraged. Yet one act of self-denial for the sake of the Gospel, one single heartfelt prayer or act of charity toward those we are called to love, will have more power in advancing the cause of Christ than months of angry listening to podcasts, or hours of sparring on social media, or years of stirring up those around us with the latest evil reports from news articles. The devil is dismayed by humility, devastated by charity, and terrified by the Cross. But when he sees Christians trying to press the works of the flesh – greed, anger, calumny, and power politics – into the service of the Spirit, he only laughs.

VI

The Winning Stance

IN DETERMINING HOW best to serve Christ in our time and place, there will be a thousand things to learn and do. Each of us will have a missionary vocation that will demand all the prudent thought and enterprise we can muster. But whatever we are doing, it can help to see the encouragement we are given concerning our fundamental stance as believers, families, missionaries, soldiers, and servants of Christ.

1. Stand Therefore

The following extended passage from Saint Paul points to the strategic importance of *standing*.

> *Finally, be strong in the Lord and in the strength of his might. Put on the whole armor of God, that you may be able to* ***stand*** *against the wiles of the devil. For we are not contending against flesh and blood, but against the principalities, against the powers, against the world rulers of this present darkness, against the spiritual hosts of wickedness in the heavenly places. Therefore take the whole armor of God, that you may be able to* ***withstand*** *in the evil day, and having done all, to* ***stand. Stand*** *therefore, having girded your loins with truth, and having put on the breastplate of righteousness, and having shod your feet with the equipment of the gospel of peace; besides all these, taking the shield of faith, with which you can quench all the flaming darts of the evil one. And take the helmet of salvation, and the sword of the Spirit, which is the word of God.* (Eph 6:10-17)

Saint Paul is giving Christian disciples a rousing battle cry, of the kind generals issue to rally their troops before engaging the enemy. One thinks of the "band of brothers" speech given by Henry V before the battle of Agincourt in Shakespeare's famous play. Yet the main encouragement Paul gives to his fellow Christians is not "Attack!"; not "Forward!"; not "Once more into the breach!"; but: "Stand!" The word is used four times in this one passage. No one doubts the importance of soldiers holding their ground and not running away, but is that the best we can do?

Paul's extended analogy is also significant. He speaks of truth, righteousness, peace, and faith as parts of a suit of armor, and armor is fundamentally a defensive measure. The one weapon mentioned for attack is the sword of the Spirit, the word of God. This emphasis might lead us to think that Paul is preparing the disciples for a defensive siege, counseling them to hunker down and dig in against a superior enemy. Yet this is clearly not the case. Paul's call to his followers was always: *"be imitators of me as I am of Christ"* (1 Cor 11:1). He is laying out for them his own strategy, which is also the strategy of Christ himself, and that strategy is anything but defensive. In all that has concerned the battle between light and darkness in which we have been implicated, God has been the aggressor. It was God the Father who started the assault on the demonic kingdom. It was God the Son who invaded occupied territory in a kind of disguise, bringing heavenly power to bear on a captive and fallen race and setting up a colony of heaven in the midst of occupied territory. Saint John wrote that *"the reason the Son of God appeared was to destroy the works of the devil"* (1 Jn 3:8). Jesus declared that he *"saw Satan fall like lightning"* (Lk 10:18). It was Jesus who provoked Satan into hand-to-hand combat and threw him down. Jesus was always on the attack and always master of events. Yet paradoxically, the spear point of his

attack was his passion and death. Jesus purposely allowed himself to be taken by his enemies, and he patiently endured the worst they could throw at him, not because he was compelled to do so, but because he knew that this was the winning strategy. *"Do you think that I cannot appeal to my Father, and he will at once send me more than twelve legions of angels? But how then should the scriptures be fulfilled, that it must be so?"* (Mt 26:53-4). By taking his stand in the will and the truth of the Father, by refusing to give up even when he seemed to be defeated, Christ completely routed his demonic foes.

Christ's servant Paul, imitating his Master, was also constantly on the attack, and he also clearly intended to defeat his enemies. He was full of energetic plans, and he stirred up activity and conflict wherever he went. Concerning his own missionary work, he wrote: *"We destroy arguments and every proud obstacle to the knowledge of God and take every thought captive to obey Christ"* (2 Cor 10:4-5). Paul was not a defensive sort of person, and though his call is to *stand*, the posture he enjoins is not defensive in a psychological or even a tactical sense. Instead, he makes clear how the heavenly attack goes forward. Christians attack the evil of the world and challenge the supremacy of the prince of darkness by refusing to be moved off their ground, by staying in the fight no matter what, and by fearlessly speaking God's word of truth even in the face of persecution and death. They imitate Christ, the great champion of truth and goodness, precisely by "standing." Why is that?

2. The Resistance

In this stage of the battle – this time between the first and the second coming of Christ, during which human souls are being sifted, sorted, and gathered into the kingdom – the Church operates as a kind of resistance movement behind the lines of the demonic enemy. Chris-

tians know that they cannot entirely overcome the curse of the Fall and dethrone the one whom Jesus regularly calls "the Prince of this world." There is a promised invasion coming, and the Church has set all its hope on the fulfillment of that promise. Meanwhile, Christ in the Church continues his work of probing hearts, gaining new disciples, stirring up loyalty to the Father, getting in the way of the devil's dark plans, bringing the dead back to life, and teaching his disciples to despise and disobey their former captor. The devil hates this heavenly society in his midst and launches desperate counter-attacks against it according to the measure of power allotted to him, but no matter what he does, he cannot snuff it out or stop its subversive activity.

Given this strategic situation, it becomes clear why "standing" is so important and why the seemingly defeated martyr rather than the externally victorious conqueror is the quintessential Christian hero. Christians always win when they stand in the truth of Christ, whatever their circumstances. Christ has arranged things for those who belong to him such that, so long as they do not give up, they *always win*. The devil knows this iron law of spiritual warfare. He knows that he cannot defeat Christians by making life miserable for them, or by stirring up persecution against them, not even by slaughtering them wholesale. The only way he can overcome them is to find a way to get them either to abandon the truth or to lose hope and quit the fight, by somehow getting them off the secure rock upon which they are standing, the rock of Christ.

Jesus taught his followers that they would grow strong, conquer, and gain a kingdom according to the pattern of his Cross: not by wealth but by poverty; not by power but by humility; not by strength but in weakness; not by coercive force but in defenselessness; not by the world's wisdom but by the seeming foolishness of God. Like

Christ, Christians triumph just when it seems that they are failing. Not that they set out to fail. Following the example of their Master, Christians attempt to be faithful, diligent, wise, competent, zealous, and patient. In doing so they are given the privilege of being channels of his grace and truth. They see God at work in their own lives and they know the joy of seeing fellow captives set free. Yet they find that at crucial times, despite all their best efforts, they seem to fail. They and their work are nailed to the Cross and crucified. It is just then that heaven's power is mysteriously released and that new life comes bursting from the grave. The Church is weakest and most vulnerable when it most relies on worldly categories of strength and success. It is strongest when it is most reliant on God and least wedded to the powers of a fallen world.

3. Presenting the Gospel in our Apostolic Age

In calling us to take on God's armor, Saint Paul writes of wielding "*the Sword of the Spirit, which is the Word of God*" (Eph 6:17). This phrase speaks especially to the task of presenting the Gospel to others. Given an apostolic time like ours, there is no easy delineation between life and evangelization. The more deeply we are converted, the more we will bring our converted selves to the task of witness. In a Christendom age, missionaries are sent off to unbelievers. In an apostolic age, unbelief is in the very atmosphere we breathe, and to conform our lives to Christ, even privately, is necessarily to bear witness to him. In a time like ours, there is, blessedly, no place to hide.

What follows are a few suggestions that might inform how we present Christ and the Christian faith in light of our current cultural world. None of these suggestions are new, but they may need greater emphasis in our time if the truth of Christ is to be clearly seen and

understood. Given the growing virulence of the non-Christian religious environment surrounding us, the job of presenting the Gospel is a mission for all of us. We need to be steadily presenting the Faith anew, first to ourselves in order to keep our minds and hearts awake in the face of the many false gospels that are constantly being broadcast around us, and then to others as the Lord gives us opportunity and responsibility: to our families, our friends, our congregations, our neighbors, our co-workers. The following list is not meant as either complete or final; it is rather an outline of certain important principles that invite further thought and elaboration.

1. The centrality of the person of Christ

   Our age has famously been characterized as being "lost in the cosmos."[26] We have no idea who we are, where we came from, what we are here for, or how we fit in to the world, and this has led to a profound sense of existential loneliness. Chesterton once wrote that while the modern world seemed to have chased God away, there remained nonetheless a hole, a longing, what he called "the presence of the absence of God."[27] The only answer to that identity crisis is found in coming to know Jesus Christ. The person of Christ is the orienting center of all reality, the immovable rock upon which we can set our feet and ground our lives, no matter how the winds and the storms may be raging.

   Christianity involves many things. It teaches a tapestry of doctrines; it involves a moral code; it presupposes a system of metaphysical philosophy; it is embodied in a complex Church

---

[26] The phrase originates with the title of Walker Percy's 1983 book, *Lost in the Cosmos: The Last Self-Help Book.*

[27] *The Everlasting Man*

institution; it has produced a long and intricate history; it possesses a rich tradition of prayer, song, liturgy, and art. Yet all these many facets are centered on one great foundation: the person whose name is Jesus. To be a Christian is to belong to Jesus, to know him, to be in union with him, to become a part of him. Everything else is encompassed in and given meaning through this encounter and communion with the living God-made-man. Christ is the absolute center, the beginning, and the end. To be rightly related to Christ is to be rightly related to everything else. Our time needs once again to be amazed and overwhelmed by Christ himself – not a system, or a theory, or a socio-political scheme, but by the Divine personality himself.

2. The importance of awakened minds

If Jesus is someone we need to get to know personally as brother, master, king, and friend, he is also someone we need to encounter as the Wisdom of God who enlightens our minds. As he himself said, he came to bear witness to the truth (cf. Jn 18:37). In our world of technical proficiency and rapid communication, our minds need to be wide awake lest we be overcome by sophisticated assaults on the Faith. An apostolic time demands of every Christian an instructed intellect. It is not enough to find in Jesus someone who comforts us and makes us feel confident about life. We also need to receive wise and vivid teaching from the One who is the answer to every question, who stands at the back of every truth, *in whom are hid all the treasures of wisdom and knowledge* (Col 2:3).

The Catholic intellectual life is a vast storehouse of riches, and in an apostolic age every priest, religious, and layperson needs to gain as much of that treasure as possible and live from it. For those who are seeking such riches, they have never been more accessible.[28] But those content to live in and from the weary world, drowsy from what C. S. Lewis called "the anesthetic fog,"[29] have never been more isolated from that wealth; a farmer or blacksmith of Christendom had more of it simply from attending the feasts and festivals of his small village or from watching the sun rise over the mountains.

3. <u>The necessity of the true narrative</u>

When Saints Stephen, Peter, and Paul first preached the Gospel, as recorded in the Acts of the Apostles, they all shared a particular method of approach: they all began by telling the story of salvation history. They preached Christ, but they did so in the context of the overall narrative that made clear his significance. The story they told was not just compelling or interesting; it was true, grounded in genuine history and real events. It was the story that encompasses every story, the story in which God

---

[28] The last couple of decades have seen an impressive array of Catholic teachers and apologists take the field, presenting the Faith with intelligence and in all its beauty and transformative power. Online projects like PrimeMatters.com, the co-publisher of this text, offer immense and curated repositories of such resources. Catholic Studies programs – graduate and undergraduate – like those at the University of Saint Thomas (MN) and the University of Mary specialize in initiating eager minds into the Great Tradition.

[29] *Mere Christianity,* "Nice People or New Men?": *What can you ever really know of other people's souls–of their temptations, their opportunities, their struggles? One soul in the whole creation you do know: and it is the only one whose fate is placed in your hands. If there is a God, you are, in a sense, alone with Him. You cannot put Him off with speculations about your next door neighbours or memories of what you have read in books. What will all that chatter and hearsay count (will you even be able to remember it?) when the anaesthetic fog which we call 'nature' or 'the real world' fades away and the Presence in which you have always stood becomes palpable, immediate, and unavoidable?*

was both the author and the main character. Much of what it means to be converted to the Christian faith is to embrace the true narrative of humanity. Our post-Christendom time has abandoned that narrative – one that was in past times often unconsciously assumed by most members of the society – and has replaced it with various narratives that attempt to situate human life and purpose in an overall understanding of who we are but that leave God entirely out of the picture. This means that we need to re-invigorate our grasp of the true story of humanity, an epic saga of high drama, which is also the story of each human person's life and the only story that will provide the meaning we are so desperately seeking.[30]

4. The primacy of mystery and the invisible world

In the Christian sense of the word, a mystery is not something we do not happen to know; it is something that we cannot know in full because it is beyond the grasp of our limited minds.[31] Thus, the Trinity is mysterious; the Incarnation is mysterious; the Eucharistic presence of Christ is mysterious; our human nature as made up of both bodies and souls is mysterious. If we are to be in relation to an infinite God, we need to be ready to face mysteries and to receive God's revelation concerning much that we could never have learned on our own. This means coming alive to the realities of the invisible world. Our proud age has wanted

---

30 An excellent starting point to (re)acquire this great and sweeping story is a small book published by ACTS XXIX, *The Christian Cosmic Narrative*. It is also available as a free audio project online at PrimeMatters.com/narrative and on any of Prime Matters' podcast channels.

31 As Frank Sheed observed in *Theology for Beginners*, "The Human Mind and the Doctrine of the Trinity": *The Trinity being the supreme mystery of our religion, this is a good moment to clarify our notion of mystery – which does not mean a truth that we cannot know* anything *about, but a truth we cannot know* everything *about.*

to abolish the idea of mystery. It resents the idea that there is anything beyond our understanding, anything that we cannot see, measure, or detect. Yet the human soul knows, somewhere in its depths, that the visible, measurable world is not all there is. As a result, our age is starving for the mysterious and the invisible. Finding ways to call ourselves and our age back to the unseen and mysterious world is an important task for our time.

5. <u>Making real what is notional</u>

Those who have grown up in a transitional time like ours often possess a good amount of abstract knowledge about Jesus and the Christian faith. They know a lot of Bible stories, and they have at least a vague sense of basic Christian doctrines. But their knowledge remains notional. It does not become the kind of real, living truth that guides the inner person and points out the way forward in life. Their hold on Christian realities is tenuous and fragile and is easily forgotten or discarded along the way. In bringing abstract notions to the point of living truths, it is necessary to engage the imaginative faculties that drive home ideas and help them to come alive. This is a key way by which notions become real. Jesus often taught in imaginatively powerful parables. He used images and metaphors that arrested attention and drove home powerful truths. The story of the Prodigal Son finds its way into our living consciousness far more effectively than a simple statement concerning God's readiness to forgive.

6. <u>The proper context: true friendship in Christ</u>

We know that the Christian faith is not simply an individual pursuit. God our Father loves us as his children and knows us

intimately: the very hairs of our heads are counted. At the same time he draws us into a corporate life that he himself inhabits. He describes us as parts of a body, as stones in a temple, and as branches on a vine. In each case, the individual organ, stone, or branch could not exist on its own. We live in a time of increasing personal isolation, where superficial relationships are the order of the day, yet the human heart longs for genuine communion with others. Christ makes such communion possible; genuine friendship is a supernatural outgrowth of the life of Christ in us. Because he has joined us to himself by inhabiting us with his Spirit, and because his Spirit is one and the same everywhere, Christians are joined to each other in ways that go beyond our natural abilities for union with each other. This opens up possibilities for a very deep kind of friendship.

In a time like ours, individuals will not often be evangelizing on their own. The most effective witness to the life of Christ will come communally. Others will be drawn to Christ by meeting a group of Christian friends, or by getting to know a Christian family, and by recognizing a deeply attractive quality among those they are getting to know. Thus, the inner life of the Christian faithful and the task to reach out to others run along similar lines. Each demands a depth of common life, to be lived and to draw others to Christ.

Conclusion: The Kingdom, the Tribulation, and the Patient Endurance

THE APOSTLE JOHN began his Revelation to the churches by reminding them of the good things they held together in Christ: *"I, John, your brother, who share with you in Jesus the tribulation and the kingdom and the patient endurance…"* (Rev 1:9). It is a telling list. He shares with them the kingdom: the worship of God, the presence of the Holy Spirit, the forgiveness of sins, joy in the hope of heaven – all the rich benefits of knowing the Lord. He also shares with them the tribulation: the good fight of faith, the necessary engagement of Christ's followers in spiritual warfare against the powers of darkness as the unavoidable condition of victory. And he shares with them the patient endurance: the strategic posture of standing, waiting on the Lord, defeating the enemy by persevering in truth and love until the appointed time and the end of the ages arrives. The posture John speaks of is true for every age and every time, but it especially comes to the fore in those times and places where the Christian Gospel is under intense attack – a time, increasingly, like ours.

What might this overall posture of standing look like?

In the face of the ravages of a fallen world, it means that Christians will cultivate a vision of faith: a calm and zealous determi-

nation to obey God, to live for him, and to cooperate with his often-mysterious strategies as he builds his kingdom. When we look out on the wide world – the political life of our country; the geopolitical situation; and the complexities of economics, digital technology, and environmental questions – we will not make the mistake of forgetting the primacy of invisible realities and so fall into thinking that everything hangs on such matters. We will not be deceived into the delusion that politics is the hope of the future, or that environmental awareness will save us, or that good economic practices are the key to happiness. We will give such questions the attention they deserve, but we will not allow them to become a pseudo-gospel for us. We will not allow habits of media consumption – the shadowy world of entertainment and breaking news – to blind us from the real world of God, the angels, and the immortal human soul.

When our gaze moves to the Church and we notice there not merely irritations and things that do not work well, but falsehood, heresy, immorality, and lust for power – serious darknesses that show the footprint of the devil – we will not be surprised or discouraged. We will keep firmly in mind the destiny and mission of the Church as the main locus of the battle for humanity, and we will not succumb to anxiety about the ultimate fortunes of the Church nor settle into anger over the sins of fellow Christians, neither of which attitude will help us to cooperate with Christ. When we face modern Judases within the Church, or when we encounter the Judas that dwells within our own hearts, we will respond like Christ: not with anger, not with anxiety or discouragement, but impelled by divine charity, with calm zeal, ready to follow the way of Christ even to crucifixion.

When we face the challenges of living in an increasingly non-Christian culture, we will remember that we have been born into precisely this age by the thoughtful providence of God, and that he has special plans to work in and through us. We will remember that there is always grace enough to deal with whatever comes our way, and we will resist all doomsaying and desperate attitudes. We will neither be lost in nostalgia for a distant time in the past, nor will we fall into the trap of thinking that Christianity is now "outmoded" and needing a fundamental change of belief or morality. Instead, we will seek wisdom to understand how Christ is responding to our times, as the Gospel of the One who is "ever ancient and ever new" continues to reach out to save the lost. We will do our best to recapture the faith-filled sight of the early Christians, who though a tiny and entirely insignificant minority refused to be overwhelmed by the power and immensity of the pagan world around them, because they knew that they were at the center of God's saving plan and that much depended on their faithfulness.

When our gaze turns to ourselves, we will keep hold of the truth that the most effective way to change the world, and the most genuine way of cooperating with Christ for the world's salvation, is to become a truly converted person. We will remember that the really strategic battle is the one we encounter morning by morning in our cooperation with the Holy Spirit as he engages and enlightens the darkness in our hearts and fans into flame the divine life he has planted in us. We will strive at all times to remember who we are: adopted and beloved sons and daughters of the King of Heaven, now living a hidden and exiled life, battling against our ancient foe, but

soon to be revealed as bearers of divine light to the joy and astonishment of all the inhabitants of heaven.

This is our time; this is the day the Lord has made; this is the age for which we were chosen; this is a time of God's energetic action as he continues to deal with the world and with each of us in love and mercy. Let us then take hold with both hands of the life and the time God has given us, in all their light and shadow, with genuine faith in our Lord Jesus Christ.

> *Therefore, since we are surrounded by so great a cloud of witnesses, let us also lay aside every weight and sin which clings so closely, and let us run with perseverance the race that is set before us, looking to Jesus, the pioneer and perfecter of our faith, who for the joy that was set before him endured the Cross, despising the shame, and is seated at the right hand of the throne of God. (Heb 12:1–2)*

About the University of Mary

The UNIVERSITY of MARY is a private, co-educational Catholic university that welcomes students of all faiths and backgrounds. The university has its origins in the St. Alexius College of Nursing, opened by Benedictine Sisters in 1915. In 1947, these Sisters established Annunciation Priory in Bismarck, a monastic community independent of the original motherhouse in St. Joseph, Minnesota. Meanwhile, the nursing college evolved into a two-year women's junior college, and in 1959, the Sisters founded Mary College as a four-year, degree-granting institution. Full university status was achieved in 1986. The University of Mary has been accredited by the Higher Learning Commission of the North Central Association of Colleges and Schools since 1968, and continues under the sponsorship of the Benedictine Sisters of Annunciation Monastery.

Since its beginning, the University of Mary has sought to respond to the needs of people in this region and beyond. Enrollment grew quickly from 69 students to about 4,000 students today. The university offers more than 55 undergraduate majors, 18 master's degree programs, and five doctoral degrees. Classes are conducted at the main campus and other facilities in Bismarck; online; at satellite locations in Arizona, Montana, and North Dakota; and at a campus in Rome, Italy.

The University of Mary educates the whole student for a full life, characterized by moral courage and leadership in chosen professions and service to the community. Every aspect of academic and social life is infused with the Benedictine values of community, hospitality, moderation, prayer, respect for persons, and service.

Already one of the most affordable, high-quality private universities in the nation, the University of Mary now offers 'Year-Round Campus,' a unique college-career option that enables students to earn a bachelor's degree in just 2.6 years and a master's degree in four years. This greatly reduces costs and allows students to begin their careers much sooner. The University of Mary offers exceptional educational value, as well as outstanding scholarship and financial aid opportunities. Within six months of graduation, 95 percent of graduates are working or pursuing additional education.

From its beginnings, the University of Mary has provided affordable and flexible degree options for working adults, today specializing in a unique portfolio of online and hybrid educational opportunities for the Catholic professional.

Nearly 470 scholar athletes at the University of Mary are formed in the vision of Greatness through Virtue and compete in 20 varsity sports through membership in the National Collegiate Athletic Association (NCAA-DII), American Collegiate Hockey Association (ACHA-DI), and the USA College Clay Target League.